Family Walks and Hikes in the Canadian Rockies

Volume 1

Family Walks and Hikes in the Canadian Rockies

Volume 1
Bragg Creek - Kananaskis - Bow Valley - Banff National Park

ANDREW NUGARA

RMB

For information on purchasing bulk quantities of this book, or to obtain media excerpts or invite the author to speak at an event, please visit rmbooks.com and select the "Contact" tab.

RMB | Rocky Mountain Books Ltd.
rmbooks.com
@rmbooks
facebook.com/rmbooks

Cataloguing data available from Library and Archives Canada
ISBN 9781771602242 (paperback)
ISBN 9781771602259 (electronic)

Editorial: Meaghan Craven
Proofreading: Peter Enman
Design: Amy Rutherford
Cover Design: Chyla Cardinal

Printed and bound in Canada by Friesens

We would like to also take this opportunity to acknowledge the traditional territories upon which we live and work. In Calgary, Alberta, we acknowledge the Niitsitapi (Blackfoot) and the people of the Treaty 7 region in Southern Alberta, which includes the Siksika, the Piikuni, the Kainai, the Tsuut'ina and the Stoney Nakoda First Nations, including Chiniki, Bearpaw, and Wesley First Nations. The City of Calgary is also home to Métis Nation of Alberta, Region III. In Victoria, British Columbia, we acknowledge the traditional territories of the Lkwungen (Esquimalt, and Songhees), Malahat, Pacheedaht, Scia'new, T'Sou-ke and W̱SÁNEĆ (Pauquachin, Tsartlip, Tsawout, Tseycum) peoples.

We acknowledge the financial support of the Government of Canada through the Canada Book Fund and the Canada Council for the Arts, and of the province of British Columbia through the British Columbia Arts Council and the Book Publishing Tax Credit.

Disclaimer

The actions described in this book may be considered inherently dangerous activities. Individuals undertake these activities at their own risk. The information put forth in this guide has been collected from a variety of sources and is not guaranteed to be completely accurate or reliable. Many conditions and some information may change owing to weather and numerous other factors beyond the control of the authors and publishers. Individuals or groups must determine the risks, use their own judgment, and take full responsibility for their actions. Do not depend on any information found in this book for your own personal safety. Your safety depends on your own good judgment based on your skills, education, and experience.

It is up to the users of this guidebook to acquire the necessary skills for safe experiences and to exercise caution in potentially hazardous areas. The authors and publishers of this guide accept no responsibility for your actions or the results that occur from another's actions, choices, or judgments. If you have any doubt as to your safety or your ability to attempt anything described in this guidebook, do not attempt it.

CONTENTS

Prairie View Trail, page 27, Moose and Crux the dogs at the crux! Scrambling down this section is tougher than going up (Courtesy Matthew Hobbs).

INTRODUCTION

About Family Walks and Hikes

Personally, I cannot think of many better ways to bond as a family than to hike as a family. The physical, mental and emotional benefits of hiking are undeniable, and who better to share and reap those benefits with than the ones you love and cherish the most?

Families living near the Canadian Rockies are fortunate to be close to some of the best hiking routes the planet has to offer. This book describes some of the more popular trips in the Canadian Rockies that are appropriate for kids of all ages. Grab the kids, get in the car and enjoy!

The challenges of family hiking

Hiking with young people has unique challenges. How do you pick the most appropriate trails for your family (see **How the trails were chosen**, below)? How do you balance long driving times with fidgety bodies? And how do you keep the kids motivated and moving once you are on the trail? Following are some tips that will help make your family hiking experience more enjoyable:

- Candy – while hiking, a treat every 10 to 15 minutes can provide the motivation kids need to keep moving.
- Bring the bikes and striders whenever possible. Kids love to bike – it's no secret!
- Learn some hiking games for kids: I Spy, scavenger hunts, Follow the Leader (with everyone taking turns as leader), Red Light – Green Light (adult controls stopping and starting of the group), "I went to Alaska with Allan and took apricots…" (place, name, food item, then onto the next letter: I went to Banff with Brittany and took baked beans…), 20 Questions, songs, and so on.
- Hike with another or multiple families. In general, kids love to hike with other kids.
- The connection humans (especially kids) have with water is undeniable. Any trip that involves water (lakes, rivers, waterfalls, creeks, beaver ponds) is likely to be a hit with the young ones.
- Whenever possible, educate the kids about the local environment and wildlife, and the benefits and responsibilities of hiking in the mountains – but don't beat them over their heads with it.
- A little bribery goes a long way. If the kids know there is an ice-cream run at the end of the hike, they are more likely to be motivated to keep going.
- Know when to push the kids and when it's time to give in – you can always return to try again.
- Have a backup plan – another hike or different activity.
- Be patient, be patient, and then, be patient.

Getting there

See the area maps on pages xix and xx. Trips in this book encompass a large area, starting at the south end of Highway 40 and reaching as far north as Bow Summit, about 40 km north of Lake Louise. All trips must be accessed by car.

Seasonal road closures

Road closures are unlikely to affect family hiking, as the restrictions occur in winter and spring. However, the closures are outlined below for those adventurous families who may want to hike in seasons other than summer.

- Highway 40 from December 1 to June 15, between Kananaskis Trail and Highwood Junction.
- Highway 66 from December 1 to May 15, west of Elbow Falls.
- Powderface Trail from December 1 to May 15, Dawson.

Facilities

Banff, Bragg Creek, Calgary, Canmore, Cochrane, Field (for Yoho National Park), and Lake Louise have all the amenities.

- Highway 1A (Exshaw): Heart Mountain Store (café, groceries, gas)
- Highway 1X (Bow Valley Provincial Park): small store at Bow Valley Campground
- Highway 1 (Dead Man's Flats): gas, motel, small grocery store
- Highway 40 (Kananaskis): many facilities, including an outdoor rental store in Kananaskis Village, a restaurant at Boundary Ranch and a gas station at Fortress Junction.

Weather

The best family hiking months in the Canadian Rockies are generally July, August and September. The temperature can reach the mid-30s in July and August, but it cools down quite a bit in September. Afternoon thunderstorms sometimes form during the hot months. Of course, snow can be expected in any month of the year but usually stays away in July and most of August. The different areas described in this book have slightly dissimilar hiking seasons and weather patterns:

- Bragg Creek is generally snow-free by April, but some areas are not accessible until May 15 because of the road closure. The hiking season goes well into October and even November.

- The hiking season at the north end of Highway 40 lasts from May to October. This area is often the best place to hike when the weather farther west is not ideal.
- At the south end of Highway 40, especially in the Highwood area and Kananaskis Lakes, snow can sometimes linger into July. September is often great for hiking here, with long periods of stable weather.
- Banff and Kootenay National Parks experience a July–September family hiking season that sometimes extends into October.
- Lake Louise and Highway 93 can have snow lingering well into July. An early season snowfall will usually end the hiking season here in early October. Routes in this area are also cloudier than others in this book due to their locations on or near the Continental Divide.

What to wear

Hiking boots, as opposed to runners, are recommended for adults on most of the trails. However, appropriate gear may differ for young children. They are generally less susceptible to the types of ankle injuries that adults may sustain. And, of course, children outgrow their footwear on a yearly (sometimes monthly) basis. A sturdy pair of runners with good tread will suffice for most of the trips described here. Kids who are up for more advanced trips (such as Fairview Mountain and Mount St. Piran) will need hiking boots with good ankle support. Bring a rain jacket and warm clothes as the weather can change dramatically and very quickly. For those hot summer days, bring sunscreen, a hat and bug repellant.

Drinking water

To be safe, it is best to bring potable water from your home, hotel or campsite. Natural sources may be contaminated with *Giardia lamblia*, a parasite that can cause severe gastrointestinal problems. At higher elevations, it is generally safe to drink from streams without treating the water. Filtering water is also an option.

Wedge Pond, page 36, heading down to Wedge Pond in the evening, on a fall day – mornings are better for the view towards The Fortress.

Wildlife concerns

Wildlife is abundant in every area described in this book. As exciting as it is for the kids to see animals in their natural habitats, it is important that all hikers try to avoid wildlife encounters. Bears, moose, deer, elk, big-horn sheep and marmots are the most common types of wildlife you may encounter, but wolves, cougars and coyotes could also present themselves. When hiking, make lots of noise to warn bears and other wildlife that you are there. Moose and elk can be aggressive in the fall, during mating season – steer well clear if you encounter them.

Of course, feeding wildlife is a strict no-no. Please discourage this tempting but very harmful behaviour.

Another form of wildlife prevalent throughout the Canadian Rockies is the tick. From March to the end of June, ticks ravenously feed on any mammal they can sink their hooks into, humans included. Check yourself and your kids very carefully after any early season hike. DEET products (for your skin) and permethrin products (for your clothes) can be used to ward off these disease-ridden creatures.

Safety tips

A few pointers to help ensure your family experience is a safe and fulfilling one:

- Hike together, especially when the kids are younger.
- Don't be lulled into a false sense of security because you are in a larger group. You still must make noise to warn bears and other wildlife of your presence.
- Carry bear spray and know how to use it.
- Consider using a personal locator device, such as SPOT, in case of an emergency.
- Stay on designated trails unless you are experienced and/or familiar with the challenges of off-trail hiking/scrambling.
- Check the weather forecast before setting out. Also, check online resources and the designated park's visitor centre for trail conditions and trail and area closures.
- Afternoon thunderstorms are common in the summer. Start early to avoid them.

Campgrounds

Camping with the kids can be a blast, a nightmare and everything in between. It is best to inundate them with camping experiences at a young age, so they get a feel for it and learn to love it.

Many campgrounds give easy access to the hikes described in this book. A few are listed here, but check the internet for a complete listing. For example, the Bragg Creek & Kananaskis Outdoor Recreation website lists all the campgrounds in the Bragg Creek area, as well as many campgrounds in other areas such as Canmore, Highway 40 and Highwood. Some campgrounds allow you to book online, but others operate on a first-come, first-served basis.

- Elbow Valley: Beaver Flats, Paddy's Flat, Little Elbow. Call 403.949.3132.
- Highway 40, north end, and Bow Valley: Bow Valley Provincial Park (as per hike on page 60). Call 1.877.537.2757 or reserve online.
- Highway 40, south end, and Kananaskis Trail: Elbow Lake (backcountry). Call 403.678.0760 or book online.

Troll Falls, page 34, Holly, Ethan, and Avarie Rosteski at the Kananaskis River, near the eagle watching area (Courtesy Nicole Lisafeld).

- Boulton Creek, Canyon, Elkwood, Interlakes, Lower Lake. Call 403.591.7226.
- Banff, Kootenay, Lake Louise, Highway 93 North: Tunnel Mountain Village, Two Jack Lake, Johnston Canyon, Lake Louise, Mosquito Creek. Book online for all.

Using this Book

How the trails were chosen

Choosing routes for family hiking is fraught with challenges. Driving time, trip length, elevation gain, and quality of the trail are but a few of the many factors you must consider and scrutinize when attempting to determine if a route is a good candidate for a family hike. Add to that the wide range of fitness levels and abilities of children and accompanying adults, and you end up with a process that is far from an exact science.

The routes in this book are mostly short, already-popular hiking trails. Preference has been given to routes that are varied and have multiple points of interest, which will hopefully keep the kids (and adults) engaged and motivated. As much as possible, routes with options to extend the length of the trip have been chosen, so that you can play it by ear and change the objective as you go. This also accommodates "advanced" family hikers who are used to longer and more strenuous trips. For example, if the objective is Saddleback Pass and the kids have no issues making it that far, you could extend the trip to include Saddle Mountain or Fairview Mountain.

In picking a specific trip for your family, the adults in charge usually know best. You may have a five-year-old who can hike every trail in this book without breaking a sweat or batting an eyelid. Conversely, your ten-year-old may struggle with even the easiest of trails. It is up to you to choose trips that best fit your family's abilities. On that note, it is always best to err on the side of caution and be conservative in choosing. As much as possible, I have tried to include short and longer hikes within short driving distances of one another, giving families the option to complete multiple hikes on one day if one hike is not enough. For example, after hiking Beaver Flats Interpretive Trail, you could stop at Elbow Falls for a relaxing rest/picnic and a very short hike; or if you arrive at Lake Louise and determine that the Lake Agnes hike may be too much for your crew, the Lake Louise shoreline hike is right there.

Trails

Parks Canada, Alberta Parks and other organizations have done an outstanding job of creating and maintaining the trails described in this book. Most of these trails are well marked and well signed. Therefore, many of the route descriptions in this book are brief, requiring very little detail. Even the routes without any signage are generally easy to follow.

Optional add-ons to extend your trip

Some trips in this book include optional add-ons, trips you can tack on to the main hike if you have the time and energy. Look for these **Going Farther** sections if your family usually has the stamina to combine adventures.

Prairie View Trail , page 27, Zeljko Kozomara captures the magic of early season snow on Mount Baldy.

Location

This section provides the driving instructions you will need to get to the start of each trip, from Calgary.

Distance

Distances represent the round-trip distance for each trip.

Elevation gain

Elevation gains represent the total height gained for each round trip, including any significant ups and downs along the way.

Difficulty and age recommendations

Levels of difficulty in this book describe conditions underfoot and the steepness of trail grades. The difficulty rating assumes good hiking conditions, so bear in mind that adverse weather or snowy conditions may elevate the rating.

The age recommendations in the difficulty ratings should be considered general guidelines. Knowing your children's abilities and limitations is key. The recommendations assume children will be able to complete the entire trip on their own two feet. If you are carrying kids in baby carriers, the recommendations do not apply.

Season

Season describes the suggested times of the year to go on each hike. However, weather (specifically snow) can affect those suggestions quite dramatically. Areas farther west are especially prone to early snowfall that can render many routes off limits, or at least unwise to travel on. Conversely, there are other parts of the Rockies, such as the Elbow Valley, that may be snow-free as early as May and well into October.

Of special interest for children

Included in this section of a trip description are recommendations for combining trips, Chariot- (jogging stroller-) friendly trips, preferable time of year to undertake the route and other tidbits that may make the trip more enjoyable for the kids (and you).

Sketch maps

Red lines indicate main trails. Dashed red lines indicate optional routes and/or trip extension routes.

Do I need any other maps?

The maps provided for each trip provide all the information needed to perform the hike; there should be no need to carry other maps. However, for those who like to carry a complete map, NTS (National Topographic System) and Gem Trek produce excellent maps for all areas covered by this book. MEC, Atmosphere and many book stores carry these maps.

If you would prefer a digital map, download the *Topo Maps Canada* app on your phone. The app uses a satellite signal, not a cell-phone signal, to pinpoint your exact location and then shows that location on a topographical map. Even if you are far out of cell-signal range the app can still determine your location. The maps on *Topo Maps Canada* also show many of the trails in this book.

Lake Agnes / Mount St. Piran, page 128, the wonderful valley west of the lake, with Mount Niblock in the background.

Doing More

If at some point in your family hiking journey you realize that the family is ready for more challenging trips than the ones described in this book, pick up any or all the following:

- the five volumes of Gillean Daffern's *Kananaskis Country Trail Guide*;
- other volumes in the *Popular Day Hikes* library;
- *Canadian Rockies Trail Guide*, by Brian Patton and Bart Robinson;
- *Classic Hikes in the Canadian Rockies*, by Graeme Pole;
- *Canadian Rockies Access Guide*, by John Dodd and Gail Helgason; and
- *Where Locals Hike in the Canadian Rockies*, by Kathy and Craig Copeland.

Prairie View Trail, page 27, Nicole Lisafeld and Rob Miller start the fun journey to McConnell Ridge, shown on left.

For those families who want to experience the Rockies year-round, consider cross-country skiing and snowshoeing trips. *Ski Trails in the Canadian Rockies, 5th Edition*, by Chic Scott and Darren Farley, and *A Beginner's Guide to Snowshoeing in the Canadian Rockies, 2nd Edition*, by Andrew Nugara, are great places to start.

The logical extension of hiking is scrambling – getting to the top of a mountain without technical means (i.e., ropes and climbing equipment). Generally, this activity is for adults; however, older children who show specific aptitude for advanced hiking may be up for it. For detailed information and route descriptions, acquire copies of Alan Kane's *Scrambles in the Canadian Rockies, 3rd Edition*, and *More Scrambles in the Canadian Rockies, 3rd Edition*, by Andrew Nugara.

AREA MAP, TRIPS 1–24

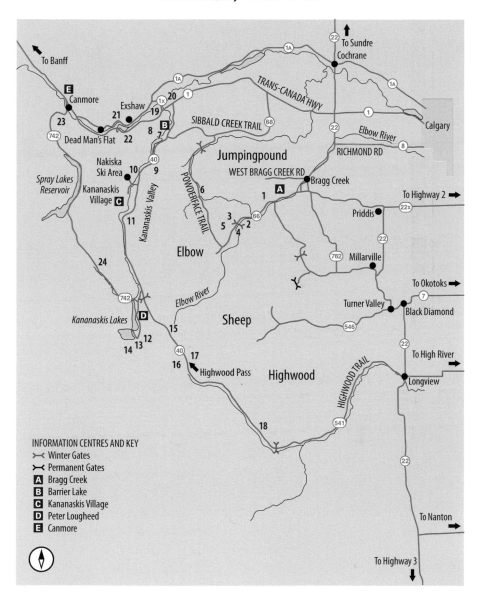

INFORMATION CENTRES AND KEY
- ⟩—⟨ Winter Gates
- ⟩—⟨ Permanent Gates
- **A** Bragg Creek
- **B** Barrier Lake
- **C** Kanananaskis Village
- **D** Peter Lougheed
- **E** Canmore

AREA MAP, TRIPS 25–42

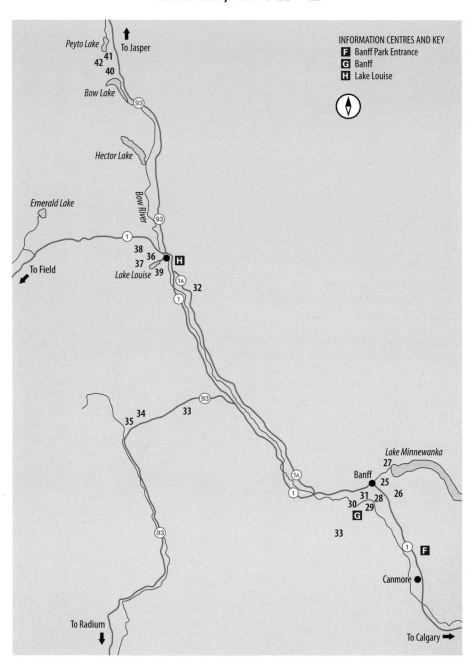

Peyto Lake
To Jasper
42 41
40
Bow Lake
93

INFORMATION CENTRES AND KEY
F Banff Park Entrance
G Banff
H Lake Louise

Hector Lake

Emerald Lake

Bow River

93

1

38
37 36
39 H
Lake Louise
To Field
1A
32
1

93

34 33
35

1A

Lake Minnewanka
27
Banff 25
31 26
30 28
29
G

33

1 F

Canmore

To Radium

To Calgary

Highway 66, The Elbow

HIGHWAY 66, THE ELBOW

The Elbow (so named because of the Elbow River) is the closest mountainous area to Calgary and therefore driving time is minimal – for the average "Are we there yet?" child, this is a good thing. The trails are excellent and generally easy to follow, with minimal elevation gain and enough points of interest to keep kids engaged. Hiking in the Elbow Valley is ideal for younger children, but older ones will undoubtedly enjoy it too.

Beaver Flats Interpretive Trail is perfect for kids of any age and is highly recommended. Older kids, perhaps seeking their first official summit, may want to tackle Prairie Mountain or Jumping-pound Mountain.

Of course, the feature hike/walk is Elbow Falls, and many families will want to stop here after doing another hike.

The quaint hamlet of Bragg Creek offers all amenities and facilities for a stop on the drive in or out.

Directions to the Elbow Area

To get to the trips in this area, drive west from Calgary on Highway 1 and take the turnoff to Bragg Creek (Exit 161). Follow Highway 22 to Bragg Creek and turn left at the four-way stop sign. You will reach the intersection of Highways 22 and 66 a few minutes later.

PREVIOUS PAGE Noah Koob, 5, at Beaver Flats (Courtesy Tanya Koob).

FROM TOP Jumpingpound Mountain, page 18, Brianne takes on baby-carrying duties on descent – in fact, she had them on ascent too (Courtesy Matthew Hobbs); **Beaver Flats Interpretive Trail, page 10,** the ponds freeze in winter. Parental discretion and supervision are required when giving three- and seven-year-olds an ice axe to play with on a frozen pond!

1. FULLERTON LOOP

*A pleasant forest walk with some terrific
views of the Elbow Valley.*

LOCATION
From the intersection of Highway 22 and
Highway 66, drive about 9.8 km west on
Highway 66 and turn right into the Fuller-
ton parking lot on Ranger Creek Road.

DISTANCE
6.9-km loop

ELEVATION GAIN
213 m; high point: 1600 m

DIFFICULTY
Moderate, recommended for children aged
five and older. Good trail throughout, with
a few steep sections.

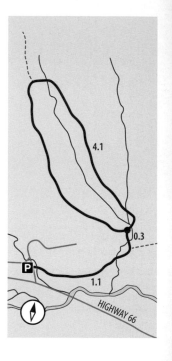

SEASON
Late spring, summer and fall.

OF SPECIAL INTEREST FOR CHILDREN
Kids will enjoy passing by and/or over several small streams and
the small rock outcrop that provides the best view of the area.

1. From the trailhead, follow the wide trail for 1.1 km, crossing
    a creek along the way and then turning left at the trail sign
    (Fullerton Loop).

2. In 300 m, the trail forks to form the loop. The 4.1-km loop
    trail can be completed by walking in either direction. Going
    clockwise will give you the best views early in the loop and is
    steep going uphill; vice versa for counter clockwise, which is

CLOCKWISE FROM TOP This little outcrop grants a full view of the area; Mary the dog, Nicole and Brian approach the steep section of the trail; Mary questions her owner's choice to go counter clockwise.

steep going downhill. There are other trails branching off the Fullerton Loop. Be sure to read and follow the trail signs.

3. After the hike, cross Highway 66 to enjoy and explore the scenic banks of the Elbow River from the Allen Bill parking lot.

2. ELBOW FALLS INTERPRETIVE LOOP

An excellent stop on your way back from a more ambitious objective or a relaxing trip in itself.

LOCATION
From the intersection of Highway 22 and Highway 66, drive about 18.6 km west on Highway 66 and turn right, into the Elbow Falls day use parking lot.

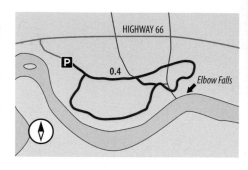

DISTANCE
0.4-km loop

ELEVATION GAIN
Minimal

DIFFICULTY
Very easy, recommended for all ages; paved trail all the way.

SEASON
Year round but use extreme care when the trail is snowy and/or icy.

OF SPECIAL INTEREST FOR CHILDREN
The trail is easy to find and easy to follow. Be extra watchful with small children, and do not climb over or under the fences. There are several areas upstream where kids can play and get their feet wet, without you worrying about them being swept over the falls.

1. From the trailhead, follow the 0.4-km loop to get good views of the falls.

2. Explore the areas upstream.

FROM TOP The falls from the trail – spot the bride and groom having their wedding photos taken; the falls are super scenic in the winter but far more dangerous – use caution; lots of activity above the falls (Courtesy Tanya Koob).

3. PRAIRIE MOUNTAIN

A very popular trip and potential first summit for older kids. Note the significant elevation gain.

LOCATION
From the intersection of Highway 22 and Highway 66, drive 19 km west on Highway 66 and park at the Beaver Lodge day use parking lot or on the right side of the road at the winter gate.

DISTANCE
7 km return

ELEVATION GAIN
700 m; high point: 2210 m

DIFFICULTY
Very strenuous, recommended for hike-loving children nine and older. Good trail for most of the trip. Rocky terrain throughout and several long sections of relentlessly steep trail.

SEASON
Late spring, summer and fall.

OF SPECIAL INTEREST FOR CHILDREN
Note the significant elevation gain here. Younger kids may struggle with this one.

1. Cross the highway and hike east on the trail just below the road.

2. After crossing Prairie Creek, take the first left up a steep trail. There is some rocky, scrambly terrain a little way up. Keep following the most prominent trail up the ridge, ignoring the other trails – they all lead to the same place, anyway.

CLOCKWISE FROM TOP LEFT Dinah Kruze tackles a snowy, January summit ridge (Courtesy Bob Spirko); Ben Hunt, 8, and Sarah Hunt, 7, at the giant summit cairn (Courtesy Ian Hunt); Finn Cohen, 6, and Noah Koob, 8, descend the upper part of the mountain (Courtesy Tanya Koob).

3. After gaining some elevation, the trail turns north and heads up at a gentler grade. Eventually, the trail starts heading in a northwesterly direction, and the grade increases. The next section is long and relentlessly steep – persevere. A few orange trail markers ensure no one gets lost.

4. After completing the heart-pounding ascent to the south ridge, the terrain opens, and you will complete the final 500 or so metres on gentle terrain. Enjoy the excellent summit view and then return the same way you came in.

4. BEAVER FLATS INTERPRETIVE TRAIL

*A unique, interesting and easy hike alongside
a chain of beaver ponds.*

LOCATION
From the intersection of Highway 22 and
Highway 66, drive 19 km west on Highway
66 to the Beaver Lodge day use parking lot.

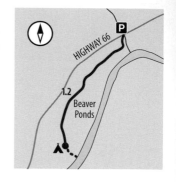

DISTANCE
2.4 km return

ELEVATION GAIN
15 m

DIFFICULTY
Easy, recommended for all; good trail throughout.

SEASON
Spring, summer and fall.

OF SPECIAL INTEREST FOR CHILDREN
Wearing rubber boots can be a good idea, as there are a few areas
of shallow water where the kids can wade. If you go in the winter,
consider suiting up with snowshoes or winter-traction devices.

1. The trail starts at the west end of the parking lot and quickly
   descends towards the ponds.

2. Follow the trail alongside the fascinating, tiered ponds, each
   separated by a beaver dam. Trying to spot the elusive and pri-
   marily nocturnal rodents will keep the kids busy.

3. Eventually a bridge takes you to the other side of the waterway,
   and you soon reach Beaver Flats Campground. This marks the
   end of the trail. Return the same way you came in.

CLOCKWISE FROM TOP LEFT This tiny peninsula is a great area for the kids. Rogan, 7, Kian, 3, and Skye Nugara, 2 (on Dad's back) enjoy a winter trip to the ponds; the work of beavers; Noah Koob and Stella Rosa Knight make good use of their Strider balance bikes (Courtesy Tanya Koob).

Going Farther

From Beaver Flats Campground, it is possible to make your way down to the Elbow River, via the D loop, for some rest and relaxation by the water. Return the same way you came in.

11

5. POWDERFACE RIDGE

The shortest and easiest route to a wonderful summit and view. With a car shuttle, it is possible to traverse the entire ridge.

LOCATION
From the intersection of Highway 22 and Highway 66, drive west on Highway 66 for about 28 km to where the highway becomes Powderface Trail. Carefully drive the gravel Powderface Trail for 5.7 km to a high point in the road and park on either side of the road.

DISTANCE
6.4 km return

ELEVATION GAIN
370 m; high point: 2210 m

DIFFICULTY
Strenuous, recommended for children aged seven and older; good trail throughout but quite rocky on the upper half.

SEASON
Late spring, summer and fall.

OF SPECIAL INTEREST FOR CHILDREN
Kids of any age will love getting to the top of this significant mountain. An ideal trip for a first summit. For the budding scramblers, there are a few rocky sections that provide some scrambling fun. Note that mountain bikers routinely use this trail, so remember to step off the trail and give them the right of way.

CLOCKWISE FROM TOP Josh and Dan scramble the cool rock at the north end of the ridge; Josh Carreiro, 10, rests on this perfectly placed rock, before the final ascent to the summit; Stacey and Cole Jones make their way to the summit – the optional high point described in *Going Farther: Two Short Options* is at just out of the photo at the far left (Courtesy Greg Jones); Josh, 10, "surfing" at the summit – why not?

1. An orange, diamond-shaped sign on a tree marks the trail. Hike this trail for a few hundred metres to where another trail joins from the left. Keep following the now steeper and rockier trail for 1.3 km (from the parking area) to a major signed junction.

2. Turn right at the junction and follow the trail up a little and then through the forest. The trail then turns uphill, and suddenly the view opens. Continue along the trail towards a col south of the summit (about 2.1 km from the signed junction). You will pass the actual summit en route.

3. An open area south of the col makes for a good rest area and lunch break.

4. To reach the summit, turn north and follow the rocky ridge to one of several high points that make up the summit. Note the trail descending the east side, if you are considering the full traverse (see **Going Farther: The Full Traverse** below).

5. There are several options for return. The best route has you continuing to follow the ridge north and then making your way back to the trail.

Going Farther: Two Short Options
There are two short add-ons for this trip.

1. For the kids who like some easy scrambling on cool rocks, instead of descending back to the trail, continue going north to where the ridge drops off on the right and becomes a jumble of solid, lichen-covered rock. Take care, as a slip over the edge would be very bad. Here, there are good views of Moose Mountain. When satiated, backtrack a little and then make your way back down to the main trail.

2. On descent, you can divert to the obvious high point to the west (see photo). There is a faint trail that leads to the top. Either return the same way you came in or, if you and the kids are comfortable on steep, loose terrain, go down the other side, taking a direct line back to the trail and the major junction below.

CLOCKWISE FROM TOP Greg, Cole and Leah Jones hike south on the ridge (Courtesy Stacey Jones); Josh and Dan negotiate the boulder field; back on the main trail.

Going Farther: The Full Traverse

And there is a long add-on! Be prepared for some extra exercise and views. Option 2 is very advanced.

DISTANCE
8.5 km from car to car

ELEVATION GAIN
432 m

DIFFICULTY
Very strenuous, recommended for children aged ten and older.

To complete the full traverse, a car shuttle is required. Leave one car at the end of Highway 66, where the road becomes Powderface Trail; park the other car per the instructions for the main hike above. After you've reached the north summit, you have two options.

Option 1: Find the regular hiking trail that descends to a point on the east side of the ridge and then traverse south back down to the road – 5 km.

Option 2: (Only for the most adventurous families, who are comfortable with route finding and steep terrain.) Stay on the ridge and follow it south.

1. Go over a boulder field and continue going south up to a treed high point.

2. From the treed high point (good views here), continue following the ridge south for a short distance. Another treed high point is visible farther south. Do not go over to this high point. Instead, turn left (east) and make your way down increasingly steep terrain to the main trail. Some route finding may be necessary here, as the trail eventually disappears.

3. Once back on the main trail, turn south and follow it back down to the road and the vehicle you parked at the end of Highway 66.

Josh demonstrates great bouldering form.

6. JUMPINGPOUND MOUNTAIN

A great first official summit for the youngsters.

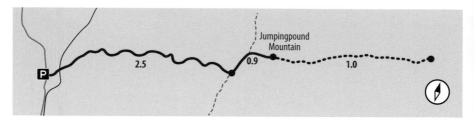

LOCATION

Highway 1 approach: drive west on Highway 1. Turn onto Sibbald Creek Trail (Highway 68). Drive about 23 km and turn left onto Powderface Trail. Carefully drive along Powderface Trail for about 16.7 km to a pullout on the right (west) side of the road. This is the trailhead.

Bragg Creek approach: from the intersection of Highways 22 and 66, drive west on Highway 66 for about 28 km to where it becomes Powderface Trail. Carefully drive along Powderface Trail for about 18 km to a pullout on the left (west) side of the road.

Powderface Trail can be exhilarating or nerve-wracking to drive. Obey the speed limits.

DISTANCE
6.8 km return

ELEVATION GAIN
417 m; high point: 2240 m

DIFFICULTY
Strenuous, recommended for children aged seven and older. Hard-packed trail for the first half. Loose rock and dirt on the second half.

FROM LEFT Sarah Hunt, 7, helps her dad geocache (Courtesy Ian Hunt); Nicole Lisafeld stops to enjoy a fine view to the west (Courtesy Shannon Young).

SEASON

Summer and early fall.

OF SPECIAL INTEREST FOR CHILDREN

Another "feather in your cap" summit that the kids will love.

1. Cross the gravel road and find the obvious trail and trail sign. Follow the trail up for 2.5 km to the next trail sign. The terrain is never overly steep, but almost all the elevation gained during the trip happens during this part.

2. Turn left at the next trail sign. Follow this trail for several hundred metres to another sign.

3. Turn right and follow the final trail to the unmarked summit, a short distance away. Enjoy the excellent view and then return the same way you came in.

Going Farther

For some extra exercise, it is possible to continue following the ridge in a northeasterly direction, over to the next high point, about 1 km away. An additional 700 m takes you to a lower high point. Return the same way you came in.

FROM TOP **Jumpingpound Mountain, page 18**, Matthew and Mera Hobbs and Crux the dog at the summit, with Moose Mountain behind (Courtesy Brianne Hobbs); **Jumpingpound Mountain, page 18**, don't forget to check out the smaller things (Courtesy Nicole Lisafeld).

Highway 40 South, Kananaskis Trail

HIGHWAY 40 SOUTH, KANANASKIS TRAIL

Driving time from Calgary's city limits to the north end of Highway 40 is only about 30 minutes, but you should expect to take 45–60 minutes to get to any trailhead. Hikes along Kananaskis Trail and in the Highwood area (Elbow Lake to Cat Creek Falls) require approximately 1.75–2 hours of driving time.

Troll Falls is highly recommended for younger children. If the kids can handle a longer drive, the three hikes in the Highwood (Elbow Lake, Ptarmigan Cirque and Pocaterra Tarn) are superb. In fact, Pocaterra Tarn and Ridge during the fall larch season is one of my favourite trips in the Rockies.

Facilities and amenities along Highway 40 are limited. However, a stop for ice cream or treats in Kananaskis Village (on Highway 40, about 26 km south of Highway 1) can be a good motivating factor for the kids. The village also has a playground. Fortress Junction has a gas station.

PREVIOUS PAGE Nicole Lisafeld takes advantage of the brilliant colours of fall at Pocaterra Tarn.

CLOCKWISE FROM TOP Rawson Lake, **page 42**, The outstanding summit view on a clear day (Courtesy Zeljko Kozomara); **Barrier Lake Trail, page 24**, the scenic rewards of spring trips; **Elbow Lake, page 45**, apparently, Elbow Lake is very popular with expectant mothers (Courtesy Matthew Hobbs).

7. BARRIER LAKE TRAIL

Minimal elevation gain and pleasant lakeshore scenery make this trip a good one for younger kids.

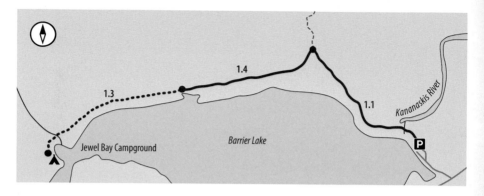

LOCATION
Drive west on Highway 1, then turn south on Highway 40 (Exit 118) and drive 8.8 km before turning right into the Barrier Dam day use parking lot.

DISTANCE
5.6 km return

ELEVATION GAIN
50 m

DIFFICULTY
Easy, recommended for all hikers; good trail throughout.

SEASON
Spring, summer and fall.

OF SPECIAL INTEREST FOR CHILDREN
The trail is mostly Chariot / jogging-stroller friendly if you stick to the main trail. Late September rewards children and adults alike with beautiful fall colours. Spring-melt trips can also be interesting, with terrific snow-and-ice scenery.

FROM TOP The small inlet, with the peninsula in front of Mount Baldy in the background; views of the lake and surrounding mountains are sweet, almost right from the beginning – note the beautiful fall colour (Courtesy Matthew Hobbs); Jewel Bay in the spring.

1. Follow the gravel road around Barrier Lake, past the dam and into light forest (1.1 km).

2. At the first signed junction, take a hard-left turn and hike the wide, undulating trail for another 1.4 km.

3. At the next signed junction, the trail turns right, into the forest. However, keep going straight, following another trail that stays close to the lake.

4. A few hundred metres farther, you reach a small lake inlet. This is a great place to stop and let the kids explore a little. Hike around to the small peninsula and enjoy a great view of the lake and surrounding mountains. If satiated, return the same way you came in. When the level of the lake is low, it is possible to hike right alongside the lake on return. However, note there is no trail and the terrain is very rocky. Consider continuing to Jewel Bay Campground (see **Going Farther: Jewel Bay Campground** below) if energy and motivation are still in abundance.

Going Farther: Jewel Bay Campground
A little extra walking gets you to a campground and additional views of the lake and mountains.

DISTANCE
Add 2.6 km return

ELEVATION GAIN
Minimal

DIFFICULTY
Easy, recommended for children aged four and older.

Continue following the main trail for approximately 1.3 km to the Jewel Bay Campground. For the best views of the area, go into the campground (being considerate of campers), and from the last campsite (site 7), make your way to the lakeshore. Exploring the rocky lakeshore can be a real treat in the spring, when the snow and ice are melting. Return the same way you came in.

8. PRAIRIE VIEW TRAIL

A longer trip for the kids that includes options to stop at the first viewpoint or go farther to McConnell Ridge and/or Barrier Lookout.

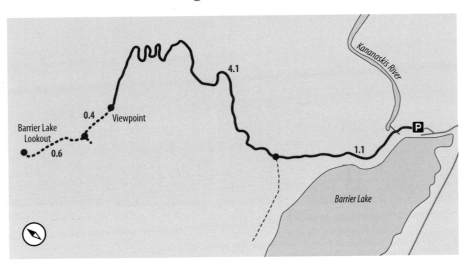

LOCATION

Drive west on Highway 1, and then turn south on Highway 40 (Exit 118) and drive for 8.8 km before turning right into Barrier Dam day use parking lot.

DISTANCE

10.4 km return

ELEVATION GAIN

400 m; high point: 1800 m

DIFFICULTY

Strenuous, recommended for children aged five and older; excellent, wide trail throughout. One or two short but steeper sections.

SEASON

Late spring, summer and early fall.

CLOCKWISE FROM TOP LEFT Crux the dog, Brianne Hobbs, Moose the dog, Heather and Max Fahr (in the baby carrier) make their way along Barrier Lake Trail, en route to the summit of Yates Mountain (Barrier Lookout) (Courtesy Matthew Hobbs); at the tender ages of six and three, Mia and Nora Skogen, respectively, complete the 400 m of elevation gain to the viewpoint (Courtesy Amy Wong); taking in the splendid view from the open area on Prairie View Trail (Courtesy Tanya Koob).

OF SPECIAL INTEREST FOR CHILDREN

Yellowing leaves make for a great fall trip. Just making it to the first open area will be a big accomplishment for young ones.

1. Follow the gravel road around Barrier Lake, past the dam and into light forest (1.1 km).

2. At the first signed junction, go straight (Prairie View Trail) and hike the easy trail for about 500 m.

3. Veer right and take an immediate left at the next signed junction. Hike the switchbacks for several kilometres to an open and outstanding viewpoint on the left. This may be the stopping point for some. If that's the case, enjoy the view, and then return the same way you came in. Continuing along the trail for another 50 or so metres provides an excellent view of McConnell Ridge.

Going Farther: McConnell Ridge

McConnell Ridge offers a slightly better view than Prairie View as well as some excellent rock scenery. The trail to the ridge is quite steep in places and requires a little scrambling.

DISTANCE
Add 0.8 km return

ELEVATION GAIN
Add 75 m; high point: 1875 m

DIFFICULTY
Very strenuous, recommended for children aged seven and older.

1. Continue following the trail as it winds neatly and steeply up the mountainside. Care is needed on some rocky, steep sections, especially when descending them.

2. Above the short, but difficult, section, a sign directs you to go left, out onto the rocky outcrop that marks the top of McConnell Ridge.

3. Be very careful while exploring this unique area. There is a straight drop down the face, and a deep fissure in the rock could swallow children and adults alike! After enjoying the view return the same way you came in or continue to Barrier Lookout (see **Going Farther: Barrier Lookout [Yates Mountain]** below). Completing the loop route via Jewel Pass, as directed by the trail signs, is not recommended for young children due to the trail's length.

Going Farther: Barrier Lookout (Yates Mountain)

A little easier but longer than the trek from Prairie View to McConnell, this add-on makes for a relatively long day for the kids but gets everyone to the summit of a mountain.

DISTANCE
Add 1.2 km return from McConnell Ridge

FROM TOP Sarah Hunt, 6, on the rocks of McConnell Ridge (Courtesy Kathy Hunt); winter view to the northwest; the lookout (Courtesy Zeljko Kozomara).

Eleven Grade 12 students from Notre Dame High School celebrate their accomplishment.

ELEVATION GAIN
Add 125 m; high point: 1981 m

DIFFICULTY
Very strenuous, recommended for children aged seven and older.

1. From the top of McConnell Ridge, go back to the trail sign and turn left onto the trail that winds its way up the mountain.

2. The trail eventually goes over to the north side of Yates Mountain, where the views start to open.

3. You soon reach the lookout. This is private property, so please respect the residents and do not trespass where posted or intrude upon their privacy. Circling around the lookout is the best way to experience the whole view. Return the same way you came up.

9. LORETTE PONDS

An easy walk around some pretty ponds.

LOCATION
Drive west on Highway 1, then turn south on Highway 40 (Exit 118) for 18.4 km and turn left into the Lorette Ponds day use parking lot.

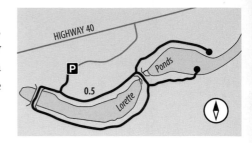

DISTANCE
0.5 km

ELEVATION GAIN
None

DIFFICULTY
Very easy, recommended for all; mostly paved trail, with a few short sections of mud trail.

SEASON
Spring, summer and fall.

OF SPECIAL INTEREST FOR CHILDREN
If the kids like to fish, bring your gear! The path is Chariot / jogging-stroller friendly, but the short distance likely negates the need for one.

1. Follow the paved path around the scenic ponds. Consider exploring the non-paved side trails too.

FROM TOP Typical views of the ponds; a great place to absorb the scenery; fall colours at Lorette Ponds.

10. TROLL FALLS

Perfect for young kids – not too long, not too short, with interesting and changing scenery throughout.

LOCATION
Drive west on Highway 1 and then south on Highway 40 (Exit 118) for 23 km. Turn right towards Kananaskis Village. Drive 1 km and turn right, into the Stoney Trailhead parking lot.

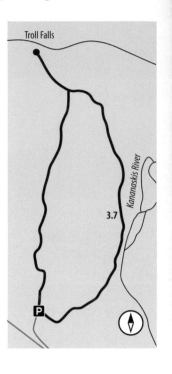

DISTANCE
3.7-km loop

ELEVATION GAIN
30 m

DIFFICULTY
Easy, recommended for all ages; good trail throughout. Some tree roots to contend with near the falls.

SEASON
Late spring, summer and early fall.

OF SPECIAL INTEREST FOR CHILDREN
Lots of varied terrain and views. Take your time and enjoy the variety. Note that much of this trail is bikeable.

1. Just past the metal gate, you will see the trail (Hay Meadow) on the right side. Follow it through forest, eventually arriving at a good viewpoint for the Kananaskis River and Wasootch Peak.

2. Continue along the trail, passing the eagle-watching area and soon arriving at two small buildings. The trail goes between the two.

CLOCKWISE FROM TOP A good view of the Kananaskis River; four fifths of the Rosteski family at the falls – dad had to work (Courtesy Nicole Lisafeld); Gavin Emanuel, 2.5, enjoys the alternate return route in winter (Courtesy Katy Emanuel).

3. Follow the trail through light forest to where it joins with another trail. Turn right onto this trail and follow it a short distance to a sign for Troll Falls.

4. Hike to the falls. Be careful when exploring the area around Troll Falls. The kids may want to scramble up to the ledge and go behind the waterfall – quite possible, but a slip would be very bad.

5. Either return the same way you came in or, for a little variety, instead of turning left, go back onto the original trail (3), go straight and follow this trail back to the parking lot. A couple of well-signed intersections along the way will guide you back.

11. WEDGE POND

*A great destination for an after-hike picnic
and/or a quick and easy hike.*

LOCATION
Drive west on Highway 1, and then turn south on Highway 40 (Exit 118) and drive for 29.8 km. Turn left into Wedge Pond day use parking lot.

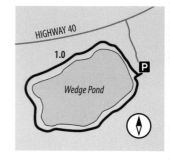

DISTANCE
1-km loop

ELEVATION GAIN
Minimal

DIFFICULTY
Very easy, recommended for all ages; good trail throughout.

SEASON
Year round, though you may need snowshoes or microspikes in winter.

OF SPECIAL INTEREST FOR CHILDREN
Early morning fall hikes are popular with children (and adults!) as they often grant spectacular views of the pond, yellow trees and The Fortress. The kids may want to get their feet wet, but the pond is likely too cold to swim in.

1. From the far east end of the parking lot find the trail that goes down to the pond. Follow the loop trail around the pond in either direction.

FROM TOP Views from the other side of the pond; Noah Koob, at the tender age of four, braves a little dip in the cool waters (Tanya Koob); Mount Kidd looks very impressive from the shores of the pond.

12. MARL LAKE INTERPRETIVE TRAIL

*A pleasant hike to a picturesque lake that is backdropped
by some of the area's finest peaks.*

LOCATION

Drive west on Highway 1 and then south on
Highway 40 (Exit 118) to the Kananaskis Lakes
turnoff. Turn right onto Kananaskis Lakes Trail
and drive 5.8 km to the Elkwood Amphitheatre
parking lot. The Marl Lake trailhead is also accessible from Elkwood Campground. Drive past the
Elkwood Amphitheatre parking lot and turn left
into the Elkwood Campground. Follow the signs
to Loop D and park in the open space on the right
side of the road between sites 114 and 115.

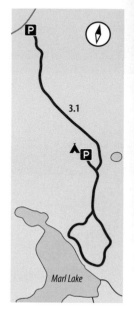

DISTANCE

3.1 km return

ELEVATION GAIN

15 m; high point: 1716 m

DIFFICULTY

Easy, recommended for children aged three years and older; excellent trail all the way through.

SEASON

Summer and early fall.

OF SPECIAL INTEREST FOR CHILDREN

The path is Chariot / jogging-stroller friendly. Remember that
morning light is the best for lake viewing.

1. From the Elkwood Amphitheatre parking lot, follow signs to
    Elkwood Amphitheatre. The signed Marl Lake Trail is behind
    the amphitheatre.

CLOCKWISE FROM TOP Picture-perfect Marl Lake and the beautiful mountains that frame it; there are other beautiful scenes along the way – don't forget to turn around for these views every so often; lake reflections of Mount Indefatigable can be mesmerizing.

2. Hike about 100 m and turn left at a signed junction. Continue along this trail for a few minutes, eventually crossing two of the campground's roads.

3. You reach the Marl Lake trailhead within minutes. Note: if you started from Elkwood Campground, the trailhead is only about 50 m from the parking area. To reach it, hike the unsigned trail from the starting point between campsites 114 and 115.

4. Follow the trail through varied terrain to Marl Lake, enjoying several terrific viewpoints of the lake and numerous interpretive panels.

5. Complete the loop and then return the same way to the parking lot, or back to Elkwood Campground.

13. SARRAIL FALLS

*Great views around Upper Kananaskis Lake
and a small but scenic waterfall.*

LOCATION
Drive west on Highway 1 and then south on Highway 40 (Exit 118) to the Kananaskis Lakes turnoff. Turn right and follow road to the Upper Lakes turnoff. Turn left, and then take the second right before going left into the parking lot.

DISTANCE
2.2 km return

ELEVATION GAIN
Minimal

DIFFICULTY
Easy, recommended for all ages; good trail all the way with a few minor ups and downs.

SEASON
Summer and early fall.

OF SPECIAL INTEREST FOR CHILDREN
There are many scenic places for a picnic near the parking lot. Exploring the lakeshore of Upper Kananaskis Lake will be exciting for kids.

CLOCKWISE FROM TOP The lakeshore is rich exploring grounds for the whole family; the kids arrive at the falls (Courtesy Tanya Koob); those who know how to use a camera can create stunning works of art with this subject matter (Courtesy Zeljko Kozomara).

1. The trail starts at the south end of the parking lot. Follow it for 1.1 km to the bridge over Sarrail Falls, taking in sporadic views of Upper Kananaskis Lake and Mount Indefatigable.

2. If you are looking for a place to rest and let the kids explore, cross the bridge over the falls and descend to the lakeshore. Return the same way you came in or continue along the trail to Rawson Lake (see next trip, **14. Rawson Lake**).

14. RAWSON LAKE

A steep hike to a beautiful alpine lake.

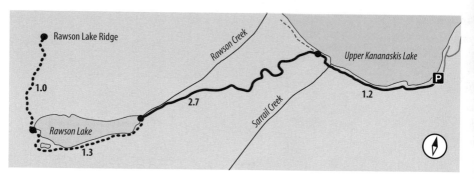

LOCATION
Drive west on Highway 1 and then south on Highway 40 (Exit 118) to the Kananaskis Lakes turnoff. Turn right and follow the road to the Upper Lakes turnoff (12.6 km). Turn left, and then take your second right before turning left into the parking lot.

DISTANCE
8 km return

ELEVATION GAIN
305 m; high point: 2027 m

DIFFICULTY
Moderately strenuous, recommended for children aged six and older; good trail all the way. Note there are long sections of steep trail.

SEASON
Summer and early fall.

OF SPECIAL INTEREST FOR CHILDREN
This could be your kids' first trip to an alpine lake! Once you are there, you may decide to gain Rawson Lake Ridge, above the lake.

FROM LEFT Sometimes you get lucky and are rewarded by a lake reflection of Mount Indefatigable in Upper Kananaskis Lake; Noah Koob, 8, arrives at Rawson Lake (Courtesy Tanya Koob).

1. The trail starts at the south end of the parking lot. Follow it for 1.1 km to the bridge over Sarrail Falls, taking in sporadic views of Upper Kananaskis Lake and Mount Indefatigable.

2. Cross the bridge and continue for about 100 m to a junction. Turn left here, onto signed Rawson Lake Trail.

3. Follow 2.7 km of sometimes steep hiking up the switchbacking trail, which leads to the lake. The impressively steep walls of Mount Sarrail tower over the lake.

4. For added exercise, exploration and great views, hike around the left (south) side of the lake on a good trail to a high viewpoint at the west end. Return the same way you came in or gain the nearby ridge (see **Going Farther: Rawson Lake Ridge** below).

Going Farther: Rawson Lake Ridge

A very steep hike to one of the finest viewpoints in Kananaskis. Definitely for experienced young hikers comfortable on very steep terrain.

DISTANCE
Add 4.6 km return from the head of the lake

Kelly Wood, Joanne Francis and Shelley Skelton hike around the lake. The route up to the ridge is near the obvious drainage at the far right (Courtesy Sonny Bou).

ELEVATION GAIN
Add 366 m; high point: 2392 m

DIFFICULTY
Very strenuous and difficult, recommended for children aged ten and older.

1. Hike along the trail around the left (south) side of Rawson Lake to the far west end.

2. Continue following the trail as it now goes steeply up to the ridge alongside a drainage. Be sure to make sure your kids are comfortable. Going down this way will be more difficult.

3. Go up to the ridge to take in the stunning view of the Kananaskis Lakes and surrounding mountains. Getting to the high point of the ridge is a difficult, exposed scramble – DO NOT drag the kids up there. Instead, return the same way you came in.

15. ELBOW LAKE

*Short but steep hike to the beautiful lake
that is also the source of Calgary's drinking water
— don't let the kids pee in the lake!*

LOCATION
Drive west on Highway 1 and then go south on Highway 40 (Exit 118) to the Elbow Pass parking lot on the east side of the road.

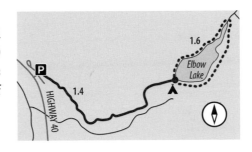

DISTANCE
2.8 km return

ELEVATION GAIN
137 m; high point: 2088 m

DIFFICULTY
Moderate, recommended for children aged four and older; good, wide trail all the way to the lake, but steep in some sections. Narrower trail around the lake.

SEASON
Summer and fall; inaccessible from December 1 to June 15.

OF SPECIAL INTEREST FOR CHILDREN;
This path is Chariot / jogging-stroller friendly, even though it is quite steep. A backcountry campground is located at the lake — ideal for the kids' first backcountry experience.

1. Hike the initially steep trail for 1.4 km to the lake. It's as easy as that.

2. You can return the same way you came in or proceed to hike around the lake in either direction. Clockwise is recommended.

CLOCKWISE FROM TOP LEFT The Stavric family at Elbow Lake (Courtesy John Doucet); Sarah McLean, snowshoeing to the lake in her third trimester of pregnancy, redefines the phrase "family hiking" (Courtesy Scott McLean); a reminder that Elbow Lake is a multi-use trail – neigh (Courtesy Matthew Hobbs); travelling right along the lakeshore on the east side of the lake provides terrific views of the lake and surrounding mountains; looks like one-year-old Aven is leading his mom, Amelie, around the north end of the lake (Courtesy Marko Stavric).

3.   If you hike around the lake, you will use a log bridge to cross the lake outlet at the far end and then continue around the other side. There is a good trail all the way, but it may be possible (and preferable) to hike right along the lakeshore. Pass through or by the backcountry campground and return to the start.

16. POCATERRA TARN

One of my personal favourites in all the Rockies.
Stunning scenery!

LOCATION

Drive west on Highway 1 and then go south on Highway 40 (Exit 118) to the Ptarmigan Cirque / Highwood parking lot on the west side of the road.

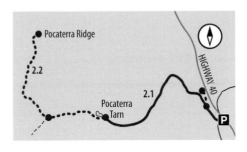

DISTANCE

4.2 km return

ELEVATION GAIN

204 m; high point: 2235 m

DIFFICULTY

Moderate, recommended for children aged six and older; good trail all the way, but some steep and rocky terrain and tricky route finding.

SEASON

Summer and early fall, especially during larch-turning season. The trail is inaccessible from December 1 to June 15.

OF SPECIAL INTEREST FOR CHILDREN

The kids will love the yellows of larch season here. You can also explore Highwood Meadows Trail (noted below) after visiting the tarn.

1. Hike the Ptarmigan Cirque / Highwood Meadows Trail north-northwest for about 300 m.

2. Turn left at the "Fragile area. Stay on the trail" sign and follow the trail up the valley. It soon trends left, into the forest.

CLOCKWISE FROM TOP LEFT The tarn; Nicole Lisafeld during the height of larch-turning season – Pocaterra Ridge is the brown-coloured summit on the right; now out of the trees, the Jones family enjoys the open scenery (Courtesy Stacey Jones).

Leah Jones, 4, and her mom on Pocaterra Ridge (Courtesy Greg Jones).

3. Be careful from here on. Several trails diverge from the main trail and lead to other destinations. The main trail gains elevation in a northwesterly direction before swinging around to the southwest, gaining a little more elevation and then levelling off.

4. Eventually the trail gently descends and then leads to the open terrain of Pocaterra Cirque.

5. Stay on the trail as it undulates through the cirque, eventually ending up at the small tarn. Hopefully the water hasn't dried up, as reflections can be stunningly beautiful, especially during larch-turning season. Return the same way you came in or continue (see **Going Farther: Pocaterra Ridge** below).

6. On your return, when you're almost back at the parking lot, consider veering off onto the signed Highwood Meadows Trail. It's only a few hundred metres long, with interpretive signs and good views.

Going Farther: Pocaterra Ridge

Fantastic scenery and views throughout. This one is for older kids.

DISTANCE
Add 4.4 km return

ELEVATION GAIN
Add 260 m; high point: 2670 m

DIFFICULTY
Very strenuous, recommended for children eight years and older.

1. From the tarn, continue following the ascending trail. Within ten minutes, arrive at an open area with great views of Pocaterra Ridge and surrounding mountains. A small but scenic stream runs close by. Some may call it a day here.

2. Continue along the trail for a short time to an important and unsigned fork in the trail. Take the right fork, which meanders up the valley in the general direction of Pocaterra Ridge. Follow the trail – it soon curves to the right – and follow your nose up to the summit and a breathtaking view. Return the same way you came in. The incredible traverse of the north ridge requires two vehicles or a very long walk back to the parking lot – not kid friendly!

FROM TOP Leah, 4, and Cole Jones, 2, at the summit (Courtesy Greg Jones); Ben, 9, and Sarah Hunt, 7, rest up before the big push to the summit of Pocaterra Ridge (Courtesy Ian Hunt); this beautiful scene is only a ten-minute hike from the tarn – Pocaterra Ridge is front and centre – the ascent route goes from left to right.

17. PTARMIGAN CIRQUE

Another deservedly popular hike in the Highwood.
Varied and interesting terrain and views throughout.

LOCATION
Drive west on Highway 1 and then go south
on Highway 40 (Exit 118) to the Ptarmigan
Cirque / Highwood parking lot on the west
side of the road.

DISTANCE
3.6 km return

ELEVATION GAIN
230 m; high point: 2438 m

DIFFICULTY
Moderate, recommended for children aged five and older; good trail
all the way. Some rocky terrain.

SEASON
Summer and early fall, especially during larch-turning season.
The trail is inaccessible from December 1 to June 15.

OF SPECIAL INTEREST FOR CHILDREN
Do not let children run ahead as a road crossing is required. Stay
together – this is prime bear habitat.

1. Hike Ptarmigan Cirque / Highwood Meadows Trail (see
    16. Pocaterra Tarn previous) north-northwest and turn right
    at the Ptarmigan Cirque Trail sign.

2. Cross Highway 40 with care – vehicles come over the hill at
    90 km/h.

CLOCKWISE FROM TOP The Boora family heading into the cirque (Courtesy Par Boora); Mia Skogen, 5, has found a great place to relax (Courtesy Amy Wong); this creek crossing is one of the more interesting sections of the loop – Kiran, 11, leads his sisters, Naomi and Cassie, 9 and 5 respectively, and Mom, Paula Boora, to the other side (Courtesy Par Boora).

3. On the other side of the road, the trail is easy to follow, though steep in places. It soon becomes a loop route that should be hiked in a clockwise direction.

4. Follow the trail through open terrain all the way up to an "End of the Trail" sign that obviously marks the far end of the hike.

5. Continue following the trail along rocky terrain in a clockwise direction. Crossing a small creek and passing a fascinating canyon is one of the highlights of this part of the trail.

6. Eventually the loop is completed. Expect to take about an hour to hike the loop. Finish the hike on the same trail you came up.

18. CAT CREEK FALLS

Kids and adults alike love this one. Not too long,
not too short, with a scenic reward at the end.

LOCATION
Drive west on Highway 1 and
then go south on Highway 40
(Exit 118) to the Cat Creek parking lot, or, from Longview, drive
west and north on Highway 541
(then Highway 40) to the parking lot. Note that from many
areas in south Calgary, the drive
via Longview is shorter.

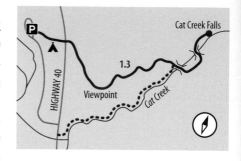

DISTANCE
2.6 km return

ELEVATION GAIN
150 m

DIFFICULTY
Moderate, recommended for children aged three and older; good
trail all the way.

SEASON
Summer and early fall; inaccessible from December 1 to June 15.

OF SPECIAL INTEREST FOR CHILDREN
Do not let children run ahead, as a road crossing is required. Makes
for a great bike-and-hike trip before the road opens on June 15,
as there is about 6 km of biking trail one way from the closed
gate. Note that both bridges were washed out in 2018. Check the
Alberta Parks website for their status before you go.

CLOCKWISE FROM TOP LEFT Leah and Stacey Jones descend open slopes above Cat Creek (Courtesy Greg Jones); Cat Creek Falls; when the water is this low, hiking out via the creek provides a scenic and easy variation for the return.

1. From the trailhead sign, hike up the trail to Highway 40. Carefully cross the highway and continue along the rising trail, up to a fine viewpoint.

2. Follow the trail along the ridge and eventually down to Cat Creek. You will reach the waterfall after crossing two bridges. Return the same way you came in. Alternatively, if the creek is low and you and the kids are not averse to rock hopping, simply follow the creek out to the road and then back to your vehicle.

CLOCKWISE FROM TOP Marl Lake Interpretive Trail, page 38, picture-perfect Marl Lake and the beautiful mountains that frame it; Prairie View Trail, page 27, the Stavric family at the viewpoint (Courtesy Artur Opalinski); Rawson Lake, page 42, clear skies are awesome for photos, but Marko Stavric takes great advantage of some blustery weather (Courtesy Marko Stavric).

Highway 1,
Bow Valley, Canmore,
Highway 742 South

HIGHWAY 1, BOW VALLEY, CANMORE, HIGHWAY 742 SOUTH

Hikes around the eastern edge of the Rockies can be reached in just under an hour from Calgary's city limits. Trails around Canmore take about an hour to reach from Calgary, and most of the hikes along Highway 742 take 1.5–1.75 hours to reach. Facilities and amenities are abundant in Canmore and, to a lesser degree, Exshaw.

Grassi Lakes is a terrific hike for beginners. The more advanced hiking family may wish to go to Chester Lake and beyond.

PREVIOUS PAGE The Moser family at Grassi Lakes.

FROM TOP Chester Lake, page 75, from above the headwall, looking down to the first tarn; **Grassi Lakes, page 71**, stunning colours of the second lake – this lake gives you a chance to educate the scientifically curious youngsters about the wonders of light refraction (is the log coming up out of the water really bent?).

19. BOW VALLEY PROVINCIAL PARK LOOP

Multiple options for combining different trails and seeing different areas of this small park.

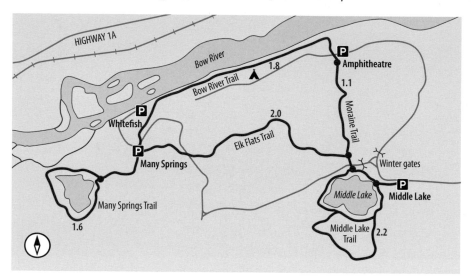

LOCATION
Driving west on Highway 1, take the Highway 1X turnoff (Exit 114) towards Exshaw, follow that road for a short distance and then turn left onto Bow Valley Provincial Park Road. Follow the road to the Middle Lake parking lot or to one of the three other parking lots (see map).

DISTANCE
3–9 km return

ELEVATION GAIN
25–150 m

DIFFICULTY
Easy to moderate, recommended for children aged four and older; good trail throughout.

FROM LEFT Middle Lake is part of a beautifully serene mountain environment no more than 10 minutes from your car; Noah Koob, 3, on the Many Springs boardwalk (Courtesy Tanya Koob).

SEASON

Spring, summer and fall. Winter trips are sometimes possible, but road access is limited.

OF SPECIAL INTEREST FOR CHILDREN

Remember to download the pamphlet for Middle Lake Interpretive Trail from the Alberta Parks web page for the trail. The highlights of the trail system here include: circling Middle Lake, Moraine Trail, hiking along the Bow River, and Many Springs. Pick and choose as you see fit. Add the Flowing Water Trail (see next trip, **20. Flowing Water Trail**) to your day for double the fun! From mid-May to mid-October there are four parking lots from which to start the hikes (see map). It is also possible to park at one parking lot, do a short hike, then drive to another parking lot for another hike within the small park.

1. From the Middle Lake parking lot, follow the trail to Middle Lake. The Middle Lake Interpretive Trail (go left when you reach Middle Lake) travels a loop through forest and is best completed with the interpretive pamphlet in hand (see note on this above). If you don't have the pamphlet, the best route is a rougher trail that goes around the lake, near the lakeshore.

Terrific views from Many Springs Interpretive Trail (Courtesy Marko Stavric).

2. Having completed the trip around Middle Lake, find Moraine Trail on the north side of the lake and follow it north, checking out the interpretive panels along the way. Pass an amphitheatre, cross three campground roads and hike to the shores of the Bow River – this takes about 20 minutes.

3. Turn left (southwest) and hike about 1.2 km alongside the Bow River almost to the Whitefish Parking lot. If possible (when the water level is low), reward yourself and the kids by hiking right on the shore of the river, instead of the trail above the river. Note that the above-river trail veers off to the left just before the parking lot.

4. Just before the parking lot, a short connecting trail takes you to the Many Springs parking lot and trail. Note the location of Elk Flats Trail here, for the return trip.

5. Complete the interesting Many Springs Interpretive Trail, also a loop, and then use the above-noted Elk Flats Trail to return to the Middle Lake parking lot and your vehicle.

20. FLOWING WATER TRAIL

An easy and varied hike for kids of any age. Good water scenery, good mountain views and a beaver pond will keep the kids entertained.

LOCATION

Driving west on Highway 1, take the Highway 1X turnoff (Exit 114) towards Exshaw, follow that road for a short distance and turn right, into Willow Rock Campground. Drive past the washroom building to the signed trailhead on the left; park.

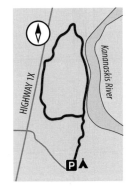

DISTANCE

2.4 km return

ELEVATION GAIN

Minimal

DIFFICULTY

Easy, recommended for all; good trail throughout.

SEASON

Late spring, summer and early fall.

OF SPECIAL INTEREST FOR CHILDREN

The trail is quite short, so take your time and enjoy the variety of terrain. Combine this trip with some or all the Bow Valley Provincial Park hikes (see previous trip, **19. Bow Valley Provincial Park Loop**) for a full and interesting day.

1. From the trailhead sign, hike 500 m (passing an amphitheatre right near the trailhead) to the official start of the loop.

2. Hike the loop in either direction (counter clockwise may be preferable, as the views downstream are slightly better

CLOCKWISE FROM LEFT Almost immediately after starting the hike, there is an opportunity to access the Kananaskis River; there are certain perks associated with being 12 kg, as Skye Nugara, 2, finds out; great viewpoint over the river.

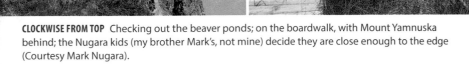

CLOCKWISE FROM TOP Checking out the beaver ponds; on the boardwalk, with Mount Yamnuska behind; the Nugara kids (my brother Mark's, not mine) decide they are close enough to the edge (Courtesy Mark Nugara).

than those upstream), stopping at each interpretive panel if desired. Early on, if you hike the loop counter clockwise, there is a beautiful viewpoint above the Kananaskis River. Hold onto small children here, as the drop down to the river is significant. Enjoy good views of Mount Yamnuska farther along the trail, as well as the beaver pond.

21. GROTTO CANYON

An entertaining jaunt up a fascinating canyon, complete with pictographs and perhaps climbers. A popular ice walk in winter.

LOCATION
Driving west on Highway 1, take the Highway 1X turnoff (Exit 114) towards Exshaw, follow that road, then turn left onto Highway 1A. Follow Highway 1A for about 11 km to the Grotto Pond day use parking lot.

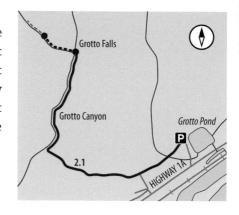

DISTANCE
4.2 km return

ELEVATION GAIN
50 m

DIFFICULTY
Moderate, recommended for children aged five and older; rocky trail throughout in spring and summer, an ice walk in winter.

SEASON
Late spring, summer and early fall.

OF SPECIAL INTEREST FOR CHILDREN
The pictographs are a highlight. Note that flash floods are possible in the canyon on very rainy days, so choose your day accordingly. This trip is popular with kids of all ages in winter, when the creek freezes. In winter, traction devices such as Kahtoola Microspikes or Yaktrax are mandatory.

1. From the trailhead sign (midway down the parking lot on the left side), hike the trail as it parallels the powerline. Follow the trail signs as you go.

The pictographs (Courtesy Par Boora).

2. If you're hiking at a moderate pace, after about 15 minutes, look for the trail sign that directs you to go right. Follow this trail into the large drainage that soon becomes Grotto Canyon.

3. Get down into the drainage (do not follow the trail that gains elevation on the right side of the drainage) and follow it upstream. There may be water flowing, or it may be completely dry. The pictographs appear on the steep walls of the canyon, about 1 km upstream. They are very faint and not easy to find – make it a challenge for the kids!

4. Follow the canyon to where it forks at a huge rock wall. Many parties will call it a day here. If you do, take a break and then return the same way you came in. Do not go up the right fork that leads to Grotto Falls; it is steep and slippery and can be very dangerous.

Going Farther: Open Terrain

I highly recommend taking the left fork at the rock wall and continuing upstream for an additional five to ten minutes, to where the canyon disappears in favour of more open terrain. At times this area teems with creatively built inuksuks. Get the kids to build one while you take a break. Exploring farther up the valley is feasible but doesn't offer much in terms of additional scenery.

CLOCKWISE FROM TOP It's winter and Nora Skogen, 3, A.J. Loewen, 9, and Mia Skogen, 6, have their Yaktrax on and are ready to enter the canyon (Courtesy Amy Wong); the Atkinson, Brown, Leskiw and Rollins families enjoy the impressive environs of Grotto Canyon – Brynn, 2, hiked all the way without assistance; a small sample of the inuksuks, farther up the canyon; the Boora family, Paula, Cassie, 4, Naomi, 8, and Kiran, 10, near the end of the canyon (Courtesy Par Boora).

22. HEART CREEK

Great for all ages. Good water and rock scenery throughout.

LOCATION
Driving west on Highway 1, take the Lac des Arcs turnoff (Exit 105) and follow the road to the Heart Creek parking lot.

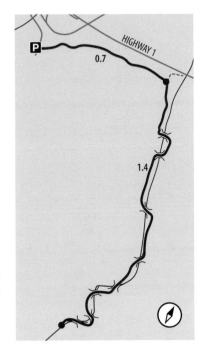

DISTANCE
4.2 km return

ELEVATION GAIN
64 m; high point: 1660 m

DIFFICULTY
Moderate, recommended for children aged three and older; good trail throughout. Some rocky terrain and many bridges.

SEASON
Late spring, summer and early fall.

OF SPECIAL INTEREST FOR CHILDREN
The numerous bridge crossings are fun for the kids, and the interpretive signs provide interesting context. Note that the course of the creek has changed slightly since the 2013 floods.

1. Find the signed trailhead at the east end of the parking lot and hike up the trail a short way and then down a big hill.

2. About 10 to 15 minutes from the trailhead, the well-signed trail turns right and heads up the valley. Enjoy the numerous bridges and try to spot climbers ascending the steep rock on both sides of the creek.

CLOCKWISE FROM TOP Approaching the section of the trail where it turns right – Heart Mountain (named for its distinctive shape) in the background; log bridges and steep rock; four happy kids at the end of the line. Mia Skogen, 6, Gavin Desautel, 11, Nora Skogen, 3, and A.J. Loewen, 9 (Courtesy Amy Wong).

3. From the right turn in step 2, it's about 1.4 km to the end of the trail, where the valley becomes a narrow canyon. There is a waterfall here, but it is hidden from view. When the water level is low, it is possible to use logs to access an area where you can see the falls, but this is NOT recommended because of the potential to slip into the deep water. Return the same way you came in.

23. GRASSI LAKES

An easy stroll to two small but fascinating lakes,
with an option to take a harder route.

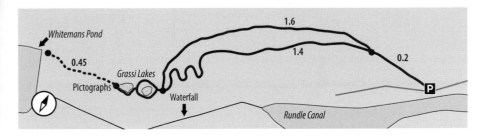

LOCATION
Drive west on Highway 1 towards Canmore. Take the Three Sisters turnoff (Exit 93) and follow the signs towards the Canmore Nordic Centre (on Highway 742). Do not turn into the Nordic Centre. Keep following Highway 742 to the Grassi Lakes turnoff. Turn left and follow the road down to the parking lot.

DISTANCE
3.8 km return

ELEVATION GAIN
244 m; high point: 1670 m

DIFFICULTY
Easy to difficult, depending on the route you choose. The "Easy" route (excellent, easy trail) is recommended for all, and the "More Difficult" route (challenging with steep steps) is recommended for children aged six and older.

SEASON
Late spring, summer and early fall.

OF SPECIAL INTEREST FOR CHILDREN
The "Easy" route is Chariot / jogging-stroller friendly up to the first lake.

CLOCKWISE FROM TOP Mark and Noah Koob at the lakes (Courtesy Tanya Koob); the big steps of the difficult route; the waterfall seen from the difficult route.

1. From the signed trailhead hike the wide trail for a short distance until it forks, at the "Easy" and "More Difficult" sign.

2. The "More Difficult" trail is recommended for older kids only, as you must ascend big, steep steps on this trail. This route is more scenic than the "Easy" route and even affords a decent view of a waterfall. If possible, use the "More Difficult" route on ascent and "Easy" route on descent. Both routes converge at the first lake.

3. Explore the perimeters of both lakes as desired, enjoying the vibrant green, blue and turquoise colours of the lakes and rock scenery. Return the same way you came in. As noted in step 2, the "Easy" trail is recommended for the return.

Going Farther: The Pictographs and Beyond

After all the terrific water scenery at Grassi Lakes, this extension offers terrific rock scenery, including some pictographs. Note, however, there is a rockfall hazard and the wooden steps are big and steep. Recommended only for older kids.

DISTANCE
Add 0.9 km return

ELEVATION GAIN
Add 90 m; high point: 1760 m

DIFFICULTY
Easy, but steep in a few places. Recommended for children aged three and older.

1. The trail starts at the far end of the second lake. Ascend the big, steep steps, enjoying the variety of rock and perhaps viewing some climbers as they ascend the steep faces.

2. The pictographs are about halfway up, over to the right. Please do not touch them.

CLOCKWISE FROM TOP The first Grassi Lake is backdropped by a climbing area (left) and the magnificent east end of Rundle; more steep stairs lead to the top; the fenced-off area where the pictographs are – one is barely visible.

3. You can hike all the way up to the reservoir at the top. Return the same way you came in. DO NOT walk back along the road as you could accidentally knock rocks down on climbers below and because of potentially heavy traffic on this narrow, winding road.

24. CHESTER LAKE

A beautiful forest hike to a picturesque lake
surrounded by stunning mountains that make this
the classic hike of Kananaskis Country.

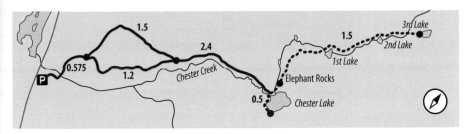

LOCATION
Drive west on Highway 1 and then south on Highway 40 (Exit 118) for 49 km. Turn right onto Kananaskis Trail, then take a right onto Smith-Dorrien / Spray Lakes Trail (Highway 742) and drive to the Chester Lake parking lot on the east side of the road. This is 1.75 hours from Calgary.

DISTANCE
8.6 km return

ELEVATION GAIN
300 m; high point: 2210 m

DIFFICULTY
Moderate, recommended for children aged five and older; good trail all the way to the lake.

SEASON
Summer and early fall.

FROM TOP The scenery opens as you enter the Chester Lake valley; there are many ways to get the family to the lake – the trip is popular with snowshoers and skiers in the winter; the south side of the lake boasts some of the best views in the area.

OF SPECIAL INTEREST FOR CHILDREN

A great larch-season trip. Be sure to check for closures due to bears in the area, and check for seasonal closures (usually May 1 to June 29).

1. The signed trailhead is at the north end of the parking lot. Follow the trail for about 575 m to a fork in the trail.

2. You can take either trail since they join up about 1 km farther on. The right option is slightly shorter and slightly steeper.

3. When the two trails join, continue up into the Chester Lake valley and eventually all the way to the lake. There are lots of places at the lake to have a picnic and enjoy the serene surroundings.

4. Consider crossing the small log bridge over the lake outlet to explore the south side of the lake for fantastic views of the area.

Going Farther: Elephant Rocks

A steep, ten-minute hike to an amazing group of huge boulders. Well worth the extra effort for the kids.

DISTANCE

Add 1 km return

ELEVATION GAIN

Add 50 m; high point: 2260 m

DIFFICULTY

Moderate, recommended for children aged five and older.

1. Hike around the left (west) side of Chester Lake until you see a trail branching off to the west.

2. Follow that trail uphill to Elephant Rocks. There are two groups of rock to explore once you get there.

CLOCKWISE FROM TOP Elephant Rocks; the rocks can be very striking in winter; the first tarn and a sweet reflection of the south end of Gusty Peak; a closer look at the huge boulders.

Going Farther: Three Lakes Valley

Even if you only make it to the first of the three lakes in this stunning valley, this is a wonderful extension of the Chester Lake / Elephant Rocks trip, in sublime surroundings.

DISTANCE
Add 4 km return from Chester Lake

ELEVATION GAIN
Add 244 m: high point: 2454 m

DIFFICULTY
Very strenuous, recommended for children aged eight and older.

1. From Elephant Rocks, continue following the trail past the rocks and then down into the next valley, less than a ten-minute hike away.

2. When you reach the open valley the trail forks. Turn right, now and head in a northeasterly direction, up the valley. Follow this trail to the first and probably most spectacular of the three lakes. Many will choose to make this their destination, especially if the kids are starting to tire. If so, return the same way you came in.

3. If not, continue following the trail around the left side of the lake, up a steep headwall to the upper valley. Here, the terrain becomes barren and rocky.

4. Hike to the second tarn (very impressive when full) and then possibly all the way to the third. You may be disappointed with the third one, especially late in the season, when it may have completely dried up. Expect to take about 30 minutes to reach the second lake from the first and an additional 20 minutes to reach the third lake. Return the same way you came in.

FROM TOP Bow Valley Provincial Park Loop, page 60, Goat Mountain and iconic Mount Yamnuska reflected in Middle Lake; **Chester Lake, page 75,** Great views of Chester Lake, late in the season and late in the day.

Banff

BANFF

Banff's lure for hikers involves the high number of easy, scenic hikes within short driving distances of one another, not to mention the townsite. No child can resist a visit to one of Banff's candy stores! Go for a hike or two, stop for dinner and then end the day with a dip at Banff Hot Springs – a perfect family outing.

Driving time from Calgary's city limits to the Banff townsite is about 1.25 hours. Parking can be difficult to find on busy summer weekends, so expect to walk a little. Note that all hikes in Banff, Kootenay Park and Lake Louise, and along Highway 93, require you to have a park pass or day pass. Either can be purchased at the Banff National Park gates, a few kilometres west of Canmore on Highway 1.

PREVIOUS PAGE Siblings at the summit. Mia and Nora Skogen at the top of Tunnel Mountain. Go Flames, Go! (Courtesy Amy Wong).

Johnston Canyon, page 101, the combination of spray from the waterfall and sunlight can sometimes cause rainbows to form above the falls.

25. CASCADE PONDS

Very short, but very interesting. Great views
of Mount Rundle and Cascade Mountain and plenty
of places to explore and then have a picnic.

LOCATION
Drive west on Highway 1 and take the Lake
Minnewanka turnoff (Exit 69). Follow the
signs to Cascade Ponds.

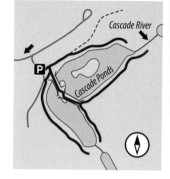

DISTANCE
0.5 to 1 km return

ELEVATION GAIN
None

DIFFICULTY
Very easy, recommended for all; excellent paved and mud-packed
trail throughout.

SEASON
Year round.

OF SPECIAL INTEREST FOR CHILDREN
After the hike, consider a drive farther up the road to Two Jack
Lake for a dip in its cool waters, or a hike around Johnson Lake.
In wintertime, this is a great place for fun in the snow. Stay on the
trail, though.

1. Explore the trails and bridges as desired. The algae in the
    ponds can make everything look green!

FROM TOP Mount Rundle reflection in the green-tinged waters of the pond; the view of Cascade Mountain from the other side of one of the bridges; the ponds look different in winter and provide a great area for snowshoeing and other forms of winter fun.

26. JOHNSON LAKE

*A relatively easy romp around a beautiful lake,
with great views of Mount Rundle and Cascade Mountain.*

LOCATION
Drive west on Highway 1 and take the Lake
Minnewanka turnoff (Exit 69). Follow the
signs to Johnson Lake.

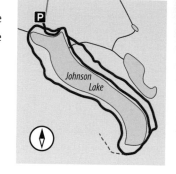

DISTANCE
3-km loop

ELEVATION GAIN
Minimal

DIFFICULTY
Easy, recommended for all; good trail throughout.

SEASON
Late spring, summer and early fall.

OF SPECIAL INTEREST FOR CHILDREN
The small beach at the northwest end of the lake is a great play/
swim/raft area. Also, paddle boarding has become more popular
on the lake. After the hike, consider a short drive farther up the
road to Two Jack Lake for a quick hike around its western shore
or for a swim.

1. Hike down to near the lakeshore and the picnic tables. The
    unsigned lakeshore trail starts here. Another trail that goes
    around the north side of the lake, but some distance away
    from it, and this trail joins up with the lakeshore trail later.
    Better to take the lakeshore trail from the beginning.

2. Turn left (northeast) and follow this trail in a clockwise direc-
    tion. The trail is generally very easy to follow. It does veer

CLOCKWISE FROM TOP LEFT Ethan McDonough and Noah Koob take advantage of good weather at the Johnson Lake beach (Courtesy Tanya Koob); geese also like to take advantage; the lakeside trail provides the best route; if you are looking for some tranquility, it often resides at the southeast end of the lake; typical activity at the lake on a hot summer day.

away from the lakeshore at times, and at other times there is a bit of a drop off into the lake – watch your little ones!

3. Upon reaching the far (southeast) end of the lake, turn right, staying on the trail near the lakeshore as opposed to the outer trail. Hike this trail around the south side of the lake and back to the parking lot.

27. LAKE MINNEWANKA

One of the Canadian Rockies' most popular lakes.
The area has lots of amenities and options to hike and explore.

LOCATION
Drive west on Highway 1 and take the Lake Minnewanka turnoff (Exit 69). Follow the signs to the Lake Minnewanka parking lot. Note that during high-traffic volume, a free shuttle to the lake is offered. To get to the shuttle parking lot, from just past the Lake Minnewanka turnoff, turn right towards Johnson Lake and look for the signed and large parking lot about 1 km along the road on the right.

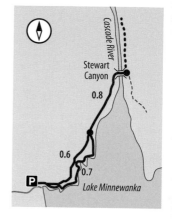

DISTANCE
1.2 to 2.8 km return

ELEVATION GAIN
50 m

DIFFICULTY
Easy along the trail, moderate along the lakeshore, and recommended for all. Excellent paved trail for a first 600 m and then a good mud trail to Stewart Canyon, and/or rocky and scrambly terrain near the lakeshore.

SEASON
Late spring, summer and early fall.

OF SPECIAL INTEREST FOR CHILDREN
The kids might like the fact that boat rentals and boat trips across the lake are available. They also might be interested in the availability of ice cream and other food items. Remember to yield right of way to cyclists and horses.

CLOCKWISE FROM TOP The rocky shoreline of the lake provides great views and fun scrambling; Keira Collins and her dad Simon Collins reaping the rewards of the scrambly, lakeside route; kayaking around the lake is a great way to experience it from another perspective.

1. From the parking lot, walk down to the lake and follow the path that parallels the shoreline for 600 m to the signed Stewart Canyon trailhead. Alternatively (recommended), from the lake, follow one of the mud trails near the lakeshore. Scrambling the rocks near the water can be heaps of fun for the kids, but use discretion. A couple of small peninsulas provide great enjoyment for all. Stay near the water until you reach a pier, and then make your way onto Stewart Canyon Trail.

2. From the signed trailhead continue along the mud trail for 800 m to the bridge that spans Stewart Canyon. Travel beyond this point is not recommended. The trail that parallels Stewart Creek going upstream offers little in terms of interest, so I only recommend taking that trail if you need more exercise. Return the same way you came in.

28. TUNNEL MOUNTAIN

*One of the easiest-to-reach official summits
in the Canadian Rockies. Another potentially wonderful
first summit for the kids.*

LOCATION

Drive west on Highway 1, take the Lake
Minnewanka / Banff turnoff (Exit 69) and
drive into Banff. Turn left onto Moose
Street. Shortly after the road turns right,
veer left onto St. Julien Road. Turn left
onto St. Julien Way. Pass the unsigned
lower parking lot (which you may need to
return to) and turn left onto Tunnel Mountain Drive. Shortly, you will reach the upper
parking lot, on the left side of the road.

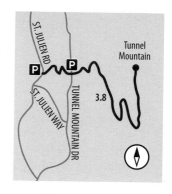

DISTANCE

3.8 km return

ELEVATION GAIN

210–260 m; high point: 1690 m

DIFFICULTY

Moderate, recommended for children aged four and older; good trail
throughout, with a few rocky sections. Fairly steep in some spots.

SEASON

Late spring, summer and early fall.

OF SPECIAL INTEREST FOR CHILDREN

The candy stores in Banff are a short drive away – a perfect
post-summit treat. Note that the east face of the mountain sports
numerous climbing routes, so DO NOT throw rocks down the
mountain.

CLOCKWISE FROM TOP Young Noah Koob, 4, looks determined as he heads up the trail (Courtesy Tanya Koob); Brianne and Penny Hobbs, with famous Mount Rundle in the background (Courtesy Matthew Hobbs); a couple of Adirondack chairs provide comfort for Mera Hobbs, 2, and Crux the dog, while they enjoy views of the Banff townsite and Bow Valley corridor (Courtesy Matthew Hobbs); winter fun atop Tunnel Mountain – Matt, Mera, Brianne and Penny Hobbs (Courtesy "Nannie" Karen Christison).

"Nannie" Karen Christison fulfills her grandmother role of protecting the young (Courtesy Matthew Hobbs).

1. From the lower parking lot, follow the trail to the upper parking lot, cross Tunnel Mountain Drive to the signed trailhead and continue up the switchbacking trail towards the summit. From the upper parking lot, simply cross the road and follow the trail up.

2. Upon gaining the upper ridge, the best views of Mount Rundle can be experienced near the precipitous right side of the mountain. A metal fence provides some protection; however, getting through the fence would be not difficult, and any slip over the edge would be fatal. Watch the children carefully here – hand holding recommended. Also, again, remind everyone not to throw rocks down the side of the mountain, as climbers may be coming up the face.

3. From the viewpoint, continue to the top, where you are granted excellent views of the Banff townsite and the Bow Valley. Return the same way you came in. For safety reasons and to avoid damage to the fragile environment DO NOT try any shortcuts down the mountain.

29. BOW FALLS AND TRAIL

Good views of a classic Banff landmark right from the start.
This trail includes options for a very short trip or a longer one.

LOCATION
Drive west on Highway 1, take the Lake Minne-
wanka/Banff turnoff (Exit 69) and drive to Banff,
down Banff Avenue and over the Bow River.
At the end of the bridge, turn left and follow the
signs to Bow Falls.

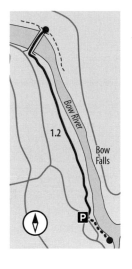

DISTANCE
2.4 km return

ELEVATION GAIN
Minimal

DIFFICULTY
Easy, recommended for all; excellent, paved path.

SEASON
Year round.

OF SPECIAL INTEREST FOR CHILDREN
Note that while Bow Falls is typically very crowded, the trail is
less so.

1. Enjoy views of Bow Falls almost immediately, at the parking
    lot. Going a short distance downstream (no trail but easy
    travel on the river shore) to where the Spray River pours into
    the Bow River offers interesting scenery and is entertaining
    for the kids.

2. After viewing the falls from various points, hike the paved trail
    up and upstream to the Bow Falls viewpoint, a few minutes
    away. Return to the parking lot or continue along the trail.

CLOCKWISE FROM TOP LEFT The other landmark mountain of Banff, Cascade Mountain, is impressive from the footbridge; the view of Mount Rundle from above the falls is a pretty good one; Bow Falls in winter; Bow Falls as seen from the trail above.

3. If you continue along the trail after the viewpoint, you will come to a footbridge over the river. Go as far as you would like. The middle of the footbridge does make for a fine viewpoint. Explore the area as desired and then return the same way you came in.

30. SULPHUR MOUNTAIN

A long, forested hike to one of the most popular destinations in Banff.

LOCATION

Drive west on Highway 1, take the Lake Minnewanka / Banff turnoff (Exit 69) and drive to Banff, down Banff Avenue and over the Bow River. At the end of the bridge, turn left and follow the signs to the Sulphur Mountain Gondola. The parking lot and trailhead appear as the road turns sharply to the right.

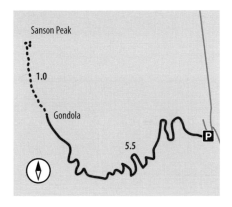

DISTANCE

11 km return

ELEVATION GAIN

655 m; high point: 2200 m

DIFFICULTY

Very strenuous, recommended for children aged 10 and older; good trail throughout, but up relentless switchbacks.

SEASON

Late spring, summer, early fall.

OF SPECIAL INTEREST FOR CHILDREN

Fun for the kids. A possible incentive to keep hiking: the free ride down on the gondola from October 10 to May 18 (as of 2018). As well, Banff Hot Springs is right up the road from the trailhead. Take your swimwear (but leave it in the car for the hike). Note that winter ascents are possible but not recommended due to avalanche concerns.

FROM TOP The wonderful view to the west; the trail in winter; the view from inside the gondola centre. (All photos courtesy Matthew Clay)

1. The trail is easy to follow and well signed. Find the trailhead at the northwest end of the parking lot and follow it up seemingly endless switchbacks to the summit. There are a couple of signed left turns you don't want to miss.

2. At the top, make your way onto the Sulphur Mountain platform and take in the views. Don't expect solitude here! There is an interpretive centre, restaurants and a gift shop inside – plenty to keep the kids occupied. Return the same way you came in, continue along to Sanson Peak (short and highly recommended) or take the gondola down (check for rates; may not be an option during peak periods; free from October 10 to May 18).

Going Farther: Sanson Peak (Cosmic Ray Station)
An easy interpretive boardwalk to the excellent viewpoint at the northwest end of the mountain. A must-do if you are already on Sulphur Mountain.

DISTANCE
Add 2 km return

ELEVATION GAIN
Add 50 m; high point: 2256 m

DIFFICULTY
Easy from the Sulphur Mountain platform, recommended for children aged six and older.

1. Follow the boardwalk to the now defunct Cosmic Ray Station (built to study cosmic rays from 1957 to 1978). Views are excellent. Return the same way you came in.

FROM TOP Noah Koob, 6, walks the boardwalk to the Cosmic Ray Station (Courtesy Tanya Koob); lots to look at from the Cosmic Ray Station, including Cascade Mountain, the town of Banff and the Bow River snaking down the valley; looking back to the gondola and the true summit of Sulphur Mountain.

31. FENLAND

*A forest- and creek-side interpretive trail
that's easy for the whole family.*

LOCATION
Drive west on Highway 1, take the Norquay/Banff turnoff (Exit 65), head towards Banff and take the second right after the turnoff into the unsigned parking lot. The trailhead is marked at the west end of the parking lot.

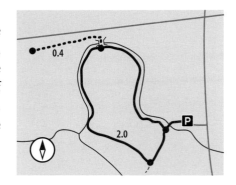

DISTANCE
2-km loop

ELEVATION GAIN
None

DIFFICULTY
Easy, recommended for all; good trail throughout.

SEASON
Late spring, summer and early fall.

OF SPECIAL INTEREST FOR CHILDREN
Bikes work well, but don't go too fast – there are many blind corners. After completing the hike, a drive down the Vermilion Lakes Road can be very rewarding. There are several piers the kids can go out onto and the views of Mount Rundle are spectacular. Another option for the family is to rent canoes or kayaks from The Banff Canoe Club (corner of Wolf Street and Bow Avenue) and sail the waterways around Fenland and into the Vermilion Lakes.

1. From the trailhead, hike the trail over a bridge and then, in a clockwise loop, follow the Fenland trail signs. Pleasant creek

CLOCKWISE FROM TOP Vermilion Lakes Road offers spectacular views of Mount Rundle; kayaking and canoeing are popular on the gentle water; Noah Koob, 6, bikes the loop (Courtesy Tanya Koob).

scenery and a few open views along the way make the hiking pleasant.

Going Farther: First Vermilion Lake

For some extra exercise – adding 800 m return – and potentially great views of Mount Rundle reflected in the first Vermilion Lake, look for the sign to Vermilion Lakes posted about two-thirds of the way around the loop. Turn left (north) onto the trail, cross a bridge, go to the Vermilion Lakes Road and hike west alongside the road for about 400 m to a pier overlooking the lake. The kids will likely want to go to the end of the pier. Take some photos and return the same way you came in. To see the remaining lakes in the group, it is best to drive to each, via Vermilion Lakes Road. The lakes sport several piers, awesome viewing points, wildlife and the mountains, and interpretive panels describing the geology of this wetland area.

32. JOHNSTON CANYON

Possibly the most popular and crowded hike
in the Canadian Rockies, but deservedly so.

LOCATION
Drive west on Highway 1, past the Banff turnoffs, and turn right onto Highway 1A (Exit 59). Follow the highway to one of the Johnston Canyon parking lots.

DISTANCE
2.2 to 11.6 km return

ELEVATION GAIN
50–135 m

DIFFICULTY
Easy to Johnston Creek's lower falls, recommended for all; moderate to the upper falls, recommended for children aged four and older. Paved trail all the way.

SEASON
Late spring, summer and early fall.

OF SPECIAL INTEREST FOR CHILDREN
Although the path is Chariot / jogging-stroller friendly, Chariots can cause congestion on the busy narrow sections, so using them is not recommended. Remind your children to walk in single file wherever possible. Expect large crowds, and be patient and considerate. Remember to allow faster travellers to pass you. Finally, and perhaps more important, usually ice cream is available at the bottom of the trail.

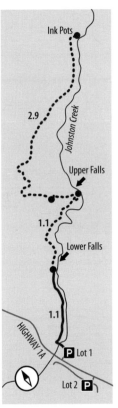

FROM TOP Gavin, 3, and Paige, 5.5, Emanuel are ready to tackle the catwalks (Courtesy Katy Emanuel); typical crowds at the lower falls. Note the tunnel through the rock that leads to another, closer viewpoint of the falls; if you are tall and/or have an infant on your back, duck! (Courtesy Amelie Doucet).

1. If you parked in the second parking lot, hike to the first parking lot. From Parking Lot 1, go over the bridge and find the trail on the other side, which goes up Johnston Creek.

2. Follow the path and catwalks for 1.1 km to a viewpoint of the lower falls. Crossing the bridge and going through a small tunnel to a closer viewpoint may be the highlight for many kids.

3. Consider walking a very short distance up the upper falls trail, where you will get a different perspective of the lower falls. Return the same way you came in or continue to the upper falls.

Going Farther: The Upper Falls

A much steeper affair than the lower falls, but still on a good, mostly paved trail.

DISTANCE
Add 3.2 km return

ELEVATION GAIN
Add 200 m

DIFFICULTY
Moderate, recommended for children aged four and older.

From the first viewpoint of the lower falls, follow the signs and trail to the upper falls. Be sure to visit both viewpoints once you get there – one at the base of the falls and the other above the falls.

Going Farther: Ink Pots

This add-on is for the older kids who have a little stamina for elevation gain.

DISTANCE
Add 5.8 km return

CLOCKWISE FROM TOP LEFT The Ink Pots – the different hue exhibited by each pool is due to the rate at which they fill – a slower filling rate means greater suspension of fine materials that absorb different wavelengths of light; the upper falls (Courtesy Katy Emanuel); a wonderful group of young people from the U.S. taking in the great scenery at the Ink Pots.

Water bubbling up from beneath the ground causes circles to form in the quicksand.

ELEVATION GAIN
Add 200 m; high point: 1645 m

DIFFICULTY
Strenuous, recommended for children aged seven and older.

1. From the upper falls, follow the signs for the Ink Pots. There is only one signed junction, about 200 m up the trail, from the first sign. Turn right at this junction.

2. Follow the trail to a high point and then down into the valley that holds the Ink Pots – a group of five small but colourful spring-fed pools, whose basins are composed of quicksand.

3. To protect this fragile environment, be diligent about staying on the trail as you explore. Return the same way you came in.

FROM TOP **Lake Minnewanka, page 88**, heading out onto one of the peninsulas; **Johnson Lake, page 86**, Two Jack Lake – Another Rockies beauty; **Sulphur Mountain, page 95**, the view to the west is not too shabby – one of the Canadian Rockies' most famous mountains, Mount Temple, is visible in the distance, right of centre; **Bow Falls and Trail, page 93**, David Emanuel accompanies his son Gavin, 2.5, down the stairs above Bow Falls (Courtesy Katy Emanuel).

Kootenay National Park

KOOTENAY NATIONAL PARK

From Calgary's city limits, travel time to this part of the Rockies is between 1.5 and 1.75 hours. Amenities are limited, but a stop in the town of Banff will allow you to stock up before your hike or get a treat on the way back.

The Paint Pots and Marble Canyon hikes are short, interesting and easy to complete one right after the other – both are highly recommended. Stanley Glacier appeals to the more seasoned hiker with good stamina.

PREVIOUS PAGE The Paint Pots is one of the most unique trips in the book, fascinating for kids.

CLOCKWISE FROM TOP LEFT **Paint Pots, page 116**, the Nugara clan at the large pool at the end of the trail; **Marble Canyon, page 114**, a couple of places at the side of the trail are perfect spots for kids to hone their scrambling skills; **Stanley Glacier, page 110**, Dan Carreiro heads up the left side of the valley, aiming for the treed plateau in the centre.

33. STANLEY GLACIER

*See the regrowth of the forest after a major fire in 2003,
a beautiful hanging valley, waterfalls and, of course,
the Stanley Glacier. A favourite hike for many.*

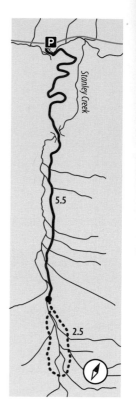

LOCATION
Drive west on Highway 1. About 25 km past Banff, take the Highway 93 South turnoff (Exit 35) towards Radium. Drive 13 km to the Stanley Glacier parking lot on the left (east) side of the highway.

DISTANCE
11 km return

ELEVATION GAIN
365 m; high point: 1920 m

DIFFICULTY
Moderately strenuous, recommended for children aged seven and older who have stamina; good trail for the first half, but rockier on the second half, with more challenging footing.

SEASON
Summer and early fall.

OF SPECIAL INTEREST FOR CHILDREN
Wildflowers can be spectacular here from mid- to late July. You can combine this trip with a visit to Marble Canyon and/or the Paint Pots (see following trips).

1. From the trailhead sign at the south end of the parking lot hike the easy-to-follow trail for 5.5 km to the signed end of the route, enjoying occasional views of the cascading waters of Stanley Creek, the luscious green of forest regrowth (after

CLOCKWISE FROM TOP Dan Carreiro arrives at the end of the official trail; Brianne Hobbs carries Mera Hobbs, 9 months, up the lower section of the Stanley Glacier trail (Courtesy Matthew Hobbs); Brianne and Mera in the beautiful valley and approaching the end of the trail (Courtesy Matthew Hobbs).

several destructive fires) and the tremendous walls of Stanley Peak on the right side of the valley.

2. At the end of the trail there are plenty of big rocks to rest upon and have a lunch break. Return the same way or continue to the upper valley (see **Going Farther: The Upper Valley** below).

Going Farther: The Upper Valley

Get much closer to the Stanley Glacier on this trail, which affords stunning views on a clear day. Recommended only for those who are comfortable on loose, rocky, steep terrain.

DISTANCE

Add 2.5 km return

ELEVATION GAIN

Add 200 m

DIFFICULTY

Very strenuous, recommended for children aged 10 and older.

1. From the end of the official trail at the boulders, trails on both sides of the valley create a possible loop route that ascends one side of the valley up to the treed plateau near the Stanley Glacier and then descends the other side of the valley, back to the end of the official trail. The recommended route is the trail on the north side of the valley on ascent, giving you the option to descend the same way or make it a loop. Also, the trail on the north (left) side of the valley is generally better and allows for almost immediate views of the glacier. That route is described here.

2. After resting at the boulders for a spell, continue up the valley on one several primitive trails through the boulder field, looking for the obvious trail to the left (north). Once you're on that trail it is difficult to go wrong.

3. Follow the trail across the side of the slope all the way up to the sparsely treed plateau. Most will call this their high point. Either return the same way you came in or, from the treed plateau, continue following the trail (faint at times) around to the other side of the valley. Depending on the time of year, this may require an easy stream crossing.

4. This trail hugs the impressively steep walls of Stanley Peak (passing a few waterfalls that become ice climbs in the winter) and then descends to the valley, back to the boulder area. From there, return the same way you came in.

FROM TOP Just above the treed plateau is gorgeous, glacial scenery (Courtesy Dan Carreiro); heading back down – the view of Mount Whymper keeps you entertained.

34. MARBLE CANYON

A short but super interesting and scenic trip,
perfect for the whole family.

LOCATION
Drive west on Highway 1. About 25 km past Banff, take the Highway 93 South turnoff (Exit 35) towards Radium. Drive 17 km to the Marble Canyon parking lot on the right (west) side of the road.

DISTANCE
1.6 km return

ELEVATION GAIN
50 m

DIFFICULTY
Easy, recommended for all; excellent trail throughout with only one section of steep stairs.

SEASON
Year round, but much trickier in the winter.

OF SPECIAL INTEREST FOR CHILDREN
Hand-hold the little ones for safety in this canyon. If the kids are up to it, you can combine this trip with a visit to the Paint Pots and/or Stanley Glacier.

1. The Marble Canyon trail is well signed, easy to follow and does not require a detailed description. It begins with a steep staircase of rock that leads to a consistently high-quality trail. Watch the kids carefully throughout. Although fences prevent direct access to the canyon, there are many places where little ones could sneak through, especially on the bridges over the canyon.

CLOCKWISE FROM LEFT The steep staircase of rock near the beginning is the toughest part of the trip; a couple of places at the side of the trail are perfect spots for kids to practice their scrambling skills; two-year-old Skye Nugara could easily sneak under the rail here – hold those hands; the end of the canyon and the trail. Travel out onto the rock by the creek Is not recommended for the kids.

35. PAINT POTS

One of the more unique and colourful hikes in the book.
Lots to keep the kids entertained.

LOCATION

Drive west on Highway 1. About 25 km past Banff, take the Highway 93 South turn-off (Exit 35) towards Radium. Drive 20 km to the Paint Pots parking lot on the right (west) side of the road.

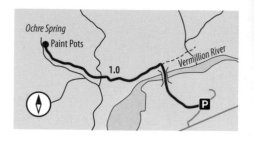

DISTANCE

2 km return

ELEVATION GAIN

Minimal

DIFFICULTY

Easy, recommended for all; good trail all the way. Stay on the trail to avoid damaging the fragile environment.

SEASON

Late spring, summer and early fall.

OF SPECIAL INTEREST FOR CHILDREN

This trail is almost Chariot / jogging-stroller friendly. Be prepared to lift the Chariot up and down the steps to the bridge. Remind your children to stay on the trail throughout. Combine this trip with a visit to Marble Canyon and/or Stanley Glacier, if you have the stamina.

1. From the trailhead, obviously leading from the parking lot, hike about 300 m down to the Vermilion River and cross it on the bridge.

FROM LEFT Use the planks along the trail to avoid destroying the environment; stay on the trail! Rogan, 6, and Kian Nugara, 3, make sure they do so.

2. Turn left (south) and follow the trail through light forest into a more open area that marks the beginning of the Paint Pots. You will immediately notice that the colour of the ground is a little unusual.

3. Follow the increasingly vibrantly coloured trail/boardwalk through the area, eventually coming out alongside a small stream. STAY ON THE TRAIL THROUGHOUT this fragile environment. The kids may want to go off trail but do prevent them. This is a good time for your best "protect and cherish the environment" lesson.

4. Interpretive trail signs, old artifacts from a mining operation, a few pools of water and, of course, the orange-tinged and iron-rich soil are highlights of the trip.

5. You know you have reached the end of the line when you arrive at an open area with a large pool at the end. The trail does continue but offers little in terms of scenic rewards until you've persevered for several kilometres up the valley. Go for the extra exercise if desired. Otherwise, return the same way you came in.

Marble Canyon, page 114, the beautiful waterfall at the end of the canyon.

Lake Louise

LAKE LOUISE

Driving time to Lake Louise from Calgary's city limits is approximately two hours. Lake Louise is deservedly one of the most popular destinations in the Canadian Rockies. Expect tons of amazing scenery but not solitude, and not necessarily a parking space. Free shuttles do run from the Lake Louise overflow parking lot (5.5 km east of Lake Louise on the south side of Highway 1) to Lake Louise during the summer months. This may be your best bet on busy summer weekends. If weekday trips are possible for you, that's the way to go.

The easiest and best introduction to the area is the classic Lake Louise shoreline hike. The option to continue along to experience the stunning environs around the Plain of the Six Glaciers exists from the end of this hike.

Reaching the summit of Fairview Mountain and/or Mount St. Piran make for great long-term goals for your family, as the children develop and improve as hikers. The ascents are great, both with breathtaking views.

The Lake Louise Samson Mall offers some amenities for hikers, including a supermarket, a book store and an outdoor shop.

PREVIOUS PAGE The Dewit family at the summit of Fairview Mountain (Self-timed photo courtesy Vern Dewit).

CLOCKWISE FROM TOP Lake Agnes / Mount St. Piran, page 128, from the small col, another "invisible" trail winds up the summit block; **Saddleback Pass / Fairview Mountain, page 135,** the wonderful summit panorama (Courtesy Vern Dewit); **Plain of Six Glaciers, page 124,** Brianne Hobbs nears the end of the line (Courtesy Matthew Hobbs); **Lake Louise Shoreline, page 122,** The ice sculptures and Ice Castle – not seen – are terrific; **Saddleback Pass / Fairview Mountain, page 135,** easy does it coming down – Hanneke and Niko Dewit, 8, negotiate the steep, loose terrain (Courtesy Vern Dewit).

36. LAKE LOUISE SHORELINE

Explore one of the most picture-perfect lakes in the Rockies, perhaps in the world!

LOCATION

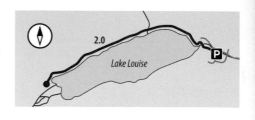

Drive west on Highway 1, take the Lake Louise turnoff (Exit 10), and follow the signs to the Chateau Lake Louise public parking lot. Note that this parking lot often fills up before 9 a.m. on summer weekends (see the introduction to this section for information about the free shuttle that runs from the overflow parking lot during the summer months).

DISTANCE

4 km return

ELEVATION GAIN

None

DIFFICULTY

Easy, recommended for all; excellent trail all the way.

SEASON

Year round.

OF SPECIAL INTEREST FOR CHILDREN

For weekend trips, arrive very early and expect huge crowds. After the hike, consider renting a canoe and exploring the lake via the water. Be sure to make the kids do all the paddling! Winter trips to the lake can be very rewarding for families, with activities like ice skating, cross-country skiing, snowshoeing and viewing the beautiful ice sculptures that abound here.

CLOCKWISE FROM TOP LEFT The classic view of Lake Louise from near the head of the lake; some take the trail, some take the rocks – Rogan Nugara, 6, and Keira Collins chose the adventure; the lake is alive with winter activities when it freezes.

1. From the parking lot make your way to the lake.

2. Hike 2 km around the right (north) side of the lake to the far, southwest end. On warm summer days, you can watch climbers ascend the magnificent quartzite cliffs. Return the same way you came in or continue up to the Plain of the Six Glaciers (next trip).

37. PLAIN OF SIX GLACIERS

An incredibly scenic extension of the Lake Louise shoreline hike.

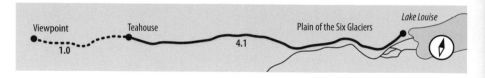

Viewpoint — Teahouse · 1.0 · 4.1 · Plain of the Six Glaciers · Lake Louise

LOCATION
Drive west on Highway 1, take the Lake Louise turnoff (Exit 10), and follow the signs to the Chateau Lake Louise public parking lot. Note that this parking lot often fills up before 9 a.m. on summer weekends (see the introduction to this section for information about the free shuttle from the overflow parking lot that runs during the summer months).

DISTANCE
14.8 km return

ELEVATION GAIN
365 m; high point: 2070 m

DIFFICULTY
Strenuous, recommended for children aged eight and older; good trail, with a couple of narrow, exposed sections.

SEASON
Summer, early fall.

OF SPECIAL INTEREST FOR CHILDREN
Recommended for older children, due to the overall length and terrain. But there is a tea house of the end of the trail for refreshments (bring cash) – a nice enticement. Note that snow can persist here into July, making travel more challenging for early season trips.

You may run into climbers on their way to the north summit of Mount Victoria (Courtesy Mark Nugara).

1. After hiking to the west end of Lake Louise (see **36. Lake Louise Shoreline** above), continue following the trail up to the valley above. Follow the trail signs for the Plain of Six Glaciers Tea House.

2. About one kilometre farther, the terrain opens, and the forest gives way to glacial moraine. In about another kilometer, the trail narrows considerably, with a steep drop on the left. A cable has been secured to the rock for extra protection against a fall. Watch the children carefully here. If this section is too dangerous, back up a short distance and find a signed horse trail that traverses below the steep section. This trail completely avoids the exposed main trail but joins up with it shortly after.

3. Follow the trail up to the tea house and stop in for bite to eat and/or drink. Explore the area around the tea house. There are some interpretive signs, benches, a few minor trails and of course plenty of views. Return the same way you came in or continue the trip to the Deathtrap Viewpoint (see **Going Farther: Deathtrap Viewpoint** below).

Fall colours and Mount Lefroy – an unbeatable combination (Courtesy Matthew Hobbs).

Going Farther: Deathtrap Viewpoint

The awe-inspiring views of a classic Rockies glacier: the Deathtrap, also known as Victoria Glacier. Recommended only for older kids.

DISTANCE

Add 2 km return

ELEVATION GAIN

Add 130 m; high point: 2225 m

DIFFICULTY

Difficult, recommended for children aged 10 and older.

Continue following the trail for another 1.5 km to a viewpoint of the famous "Deathtrap" – the steep tongue of the Victoria Glacier known for avalanches and deep, hidden crevasses. The trail loses elevation and then regains it alongside the moraine of the glacier, eventually ending when the terrain gets too steep. Enjoy the view of the Deathtrap leading up to Abbott Pass (and hut), Mounts Aberdeen, Lefroy, and Victoria, and The Mitre, and then return the same way you came in.

CLOCKWISE FROM TOP Coming up the moraine (Courtesy Brigid Meegan Scott); Brianne Hobbs near the end of the line (Courtesy Matthew Hobbs); winter trips can be stunning, but are extremely strenuous.

38. LAKE AGNES / MOUNT ST. PIRAN

Start at one stunning lake and end up at another
– a great trip for the whole family.

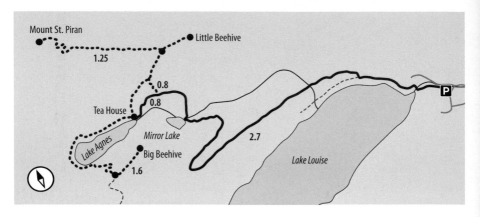

LOCATION

Drive west on Highway 1, take the Lake Louise turnoff (Exit 10), and follow the signs to the Chateau Lake Louise public parking lot. Note that this parking lot often fills up before 9 a.m. on summer weekends (see the introduction to this section for information about the free shuttle from the overflow parking lot that runs during the summer months).

DISTANCE

7 km return (Lake Agnes)

ELEVATION GAIN

400 m; high point: 2135 m

DIFFICULTY

Strenuous, recommended for children aged six and older; excellent trail all the way.

SEASON

Summer and early fall.

CLOCKWISE FROM TOP Lake Agnes – early morning trips are often rewarded with relative solitude and stunning lake reflections – note the Devil's Thumb rock formations at the left, for those **Going Farther: Big Beehive**; a small waterfall immediately below Lake Agnes and Big Beehive (Courtesy Vern Dewit); Big Beehive above Mirror Lake (Courtesy Vern Dewit).

Misty morning view from Little Beehive.

OF SPECIAL INTEREST FOR CHILDREN
The kids will love the yellows of larch season here. Make sure you go early to avoid the crowds. Finally, entice your kids to persevere with the promise of refreshments at the Lake Agnes Tea House.

1. From the parking lot, make your way to the lake via the connecting trail and start hiking around the right (north) side of the lake. Find the signs for Lake Agnes and follow the relatively gently graded trail for 2.7 km to the first stop at Mirror Lake.

2. After checking out Mirror Lake, return to the Lake Agnes trail and follow it for 0.8 km to Lake Agnes, passing a signed junction for Little Beehive along the way. Keep following the signs to Lake Agnes. Upon arriving, you will encounter the tea house immediately; it sits at the far east end of the lake.

3. Either go back the same way you came in or extend the trip by hiking around the right (north) side of the lake to the west end. Here, you will be treated to an excellent view of the lake and the surrounding mountains. From the west end there is also a trail that heads west, up into the stunning valley under Mounts Niblock and Whyte. Follow that trail for as long as desired and then return the same way you came in.

Going Farther: Little Beehive
A little extra exercise with a few fantastic views along the way.

Great self-timed photo with Brigid Meegan Scott and Mark Scott, taken by Brigid, on the way to Little Beehive.

DISTANCE
Add 2.2 km return

ELEVATION GAIN
Add 105 m; high point: 2240 m

DIFFICULTY
Strenuous, recommended for children aged nine and older.

1. From near the Lake Agnes Tea House, follow the signs for Little Beehive. Note that it is not necessary to backtrack to the junction you passed on the way up. As well, note that if you intend to ascend Mount St. Piran after Little Beehive, remember the location of the trail sign for Mount St. Piran that occurs about halfway to Little Beehive.

2. The best views occur shortly after passing the trail sign mentioned above. Look for an open area to the right (south) where you can venture out onto the rock. There is a significant drop, so hold onto the young ones. The views across the valley are awesome.

3. From the end of the trail (at a decommissioned fire lookout) you will have to wander around a little to experience views in different directions. Return the same way, initially. You don't have to go back to Lake Agnes. Follow the signs for the alternate trail back down to Mirror Lake and out. Mount St. Piran is also an option from Little Beehive – remember the location of that trail sign noted in step 1.

Going Farther: Mount St. Piran

A serious summit with a seriously amazing view! Recommended only for older kids with sturdy footwear.

DISTANCE
Add 5.7 km return from Lake Agnes

ELEVATION GAIN
Add 500 m from Lake Agnes; high point: 2633 m

DIFFICULTY
Very strenuous, recommended for children aged 12 and older.

1. From Lake Agnes, follow the signs to Little Beehive for about 500 m.

2. Look for a trail sign that informally marks the Mount St. Piran trail (as of 2018, "St. Piran" was scribbled on the official sign with felt pen). Turn left onto this trail and follow it in a westerly direction for about 10 minutes, through forest to the open slopes of Mount St. Piran.

3. The trail very neatly switchbacks up the entire mountain. Before the final ascent, you will arrive at the small col, with a terrific view to the north and east.

4. Follow the trail all the way to the expansive summit. The three lakes (Agnes, Louise and Mirror) are not visible from the summit; however, a short loss of elevation towards Lake Louise reveals a stunning view of all three. Return the same way you

Getting this view of the three lakes requires a minor elevation loss to the southeast.

came in. There is an alternate descent route via the St. Piran / Niblock col; however, it is NOT recommended for families.

Going Farther: Big Beehive

A scenic jaunt around the lake and then up to a decent viewpoint above it.

DISTANCE

Add 3.2 km return

ELEVATION GAIN

Add 135 m; high point: 2270 m

DIFFICULTY

Strenuous, recommended for children aged nine and older.

1. From Lake Agnes, follow the signs and trail around the right side of the lake, around to the south side and then up a series of steep switchbacks to the col between Big Beehive and Devil's Thumb, the prominent and very distinctively shaped formation of rock west of the Big Beehive.

2. Turn left (east) and follow the trail to the shelter at the top of Big Beehive. Trees do block some of the views and so some movement around the summit is required to take it all in. Return the same way you came in or take an alternate descent route back down to Mirror Lake, as indicated by the signs.

CLOCKWISE FROM TOP On the Big Beehive trail, looking back to Lake Agnes and Mount St. Piran; view from the shelter; the view of the outrageously beautiful Lefroy and Victoria; sweet golden larches line the switchbacks. (All photos courtesy Vern Dewit)

39. SADDLEBACK PASS / FAIRVIEW MOUNTAIN

*A scenic and steep grind to a beautiful pass
and the gateway to one of the finest viewpoints
in the Rockies, atop Fairview Mountain.*

LOCATION
Drive west on Highway 1, take the Lake Louise turnoff (Exit 10), and follow the signs to the Chateau Lake Louise public parking lot. Note that this parking lot often fills up before 9 a.m. on summer weekends (see the introduction to this section for information about the free shuttle from the overflow parking lot that runs during the summer months).

DISTANCE
7.4 km return (Saddleback Pass)

ELEVATION GAIN
595 m; high point: 2315 m

DIFFICULTY
Strenuous, recommended for children aged eight and older; good trail up to the hanging valley. Steep, rocky trail to the summit of Fairview and Saddle Mountain.

SEASON
Summer and early fall.

OF SPECIAL INTEREST FOR CHILDREN
Lots of larches grow at the pass, so late-September trips can be super scenic. There are options to reach the summit of Fairview Mountain and/or Saddle Mountain if Saddleback Pass is not enough for you and the kids.

Niko, 8, Hanneke and Kaycie Dewit, 10, leading the way, on the Saddleback Pass trail (Courtesy Vern Dewit).

1. From the parking lot, make your way to the lake and find the trail sign for Saddleback Pass on the left (northeast) side of the lake.

2. The route to the pass is well signed and easy to follow. Gaining the pass to the sight of Sheol Mountain and the beautiful Haddo Peak can be a wonderful experience. Return the same way you came in or continue along to Fairview Mountain and/ or Saddle Mountain, per the **Going Farther** suggestions below.

Going Farther: Fairview Mountain

With over 1000 m of elevation gain from the Lake Louise parking lot, this is the toughest ascent in the book for kids. It also sports perhaps the best summit view of any trip in the book – pick a clear day!

DISTANCE
Add 2.8 km return from Saddleback Pass

ELEVATION GAIN
Add 410 m; high point: 2744 m

The Dewit family at Saddleback Pass. Sheol Mountain, left, and Haddo Peak, right (Courtesy Vern Dewit).

DIFFICULTY

Very strenuous, recommended for children aged 12 and older.

OF SPECIAL INTEREST FOR CHILDREN

Recommended for older children, due to the overall length, significant elevation gain and rocky terrain. Sturdy footwear is a must. Snow can remain on the ascent slopes into July. Go later in the summer to avoid travel on snow.

1. From Saddleback Pass, the route up Fairview Mountain, to the northwest, is obvious and easy to follow. A good trail goes all the way to the summit. Monitor the kids carefully on this one and make sure they will be comfortable descending the steep and sometimes loose trail.

2. Take in the spectacular summit view and then return the same way you came in. True masochists will run up Saddle Mountain once back at Saddleback Pass.

Kaycie Dewit, 10, leads the route up Fairview Mountain (Courtesy Vern Dewit).

Going (Even) Farther: Saddle Mountain

Saddle Mountain can be easily ascended in conjunction with Fairview or as an alternative to Fairview, if that ascent is too much for the kids. The view pales in comparison to that from Fairview but is still outstanding.

DISTANCE

Add 1 km return from Saddleback Pass

ELEVATION GAIN

Add 130 m; high point: 2433 m

DIFFICULTY

Strenuous, recommended for children aged 10 and older.

1. From Saddleback Pass, the route up Saddle Mountain, to the east, is also obvious (see photo). Gain the ridge and then follow it to the summit. Do not stray too far to the right (south), as huge rock bands line the south face. The rocky terrain does make this ascent a little challenging for younger kids.

2. Enjoy the terrific view of Mount Temple, Sheol Mountain and Haddo Peak and then return the same way you came in.

CLOCKWISE FROM TOP LEFT Noah Koob, 2 at the time, knows good rock when he lies on it – awesome quartzite! (Courtesy Tanya Koob); what a view – Danica Marks, 10, Anibel Erickson, 10 (back row), Abishai Erickson, 8 (middle row), Noah Koob, 7, Esme Erickson, 6, and Sebastian Marks, 8 (front row) have good reason to celebrate this achievement (Courtesy Alyssa Erickson); Saddle Mountain as seen from near Saddleback Pass – the easiest ascent route goes around to the right (Courtesy Vern Dewit).

CLOCKWISE FROM TOP LEFT Lake Agnes / Mount St. Piran, page 128, looking back over the lake from the west end; **Lake Louise Shoreline, page 122**, Rogan Nugara, 6, and Keira Collins chose the adventure; **Saddleback Pass / Fairview Mountain, page 135**, winter ascents of Saddle can be breathtaking, but are considerably more dangerous due to avalanches – you'll have to wait until you have AST (avalanche skills training) 1 or 2, kids; **Lake Agnes / Mount St. Piran, page 128**, stunning view of mounts Niblock and Whyte from the summit of St. Piran.

Icefields Parkway
(Highway 93 North)

ICEFIELDS PARKWAY (HIGHWAY 93 NORTH)

Hopefully, the longer driving time (2.5 hours) will not deter families from making their way to Highway 93 North. The road has deservedly been described as one of the most scenic drives in the world. Bow Lake is simply stunning, and the Bow Glacier Falls hike is one of my all-time Rockies favourites. Numerous other worthy hikes occur along this road that may appear in subsequent editions of the *Popular Day Hikes* series.

There are no amenities on the southern half of Highway 93 North. Stop at Lake Louise if needed.

PREVIOUS PAGE Tanya and Noah Koob, 7, are rewarded with a terrific view of Bow Lake from Bow Summit (Courtesy Mark Koob).

CLOCKWISE FROM TOP Peyto Lake Viewpoints, page 147, Noah Koob (age eight) drinks in the view from near the upper viewpoint (Courtesy Tanya Koob); **Bow Glacier Falls, page 144**, getting up close to Bow Glacier Falls; **Peyto Lake Viewpoints, page 147**, the rock pile by the lake grants terrific views.

40. BOW GLACIER FALLS

One of the most beautiful lakes in the Rockies – period!
And you get to see a stunning waterfall too.

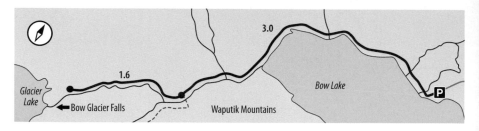

LOCATION

Drive west on Highway 1, past Lake Louise, and take the Highway 93 turnoff (Exit 7) towards Jasper. Drive about 36 km and turn left into the Bow Lake (Num-Ti-Jah Lodge) parking lot.

DISTANCE

9.2 km return

ELEVATION GAIN

135 m; high point: 2080 m

DIFFICULTY

Moderately difficult, recommended for children aged seven and older; varied terrain underfoot: mud trail, some tree roots in one section, steep stairs, and rocky terrain before the falls. Expect to do a little boulder-hopping too.

SEASON

Summer and early fall.

OF SPECIAL INTEREST FOR CHILDREN

Even the simple hike around the northwest side of Bow Lake makes for a worthwhile trip, especially on a clear, calm day. Kids will love the colour of the lake. Early morning trips are preferable for lake reflections and morning to early afternoon for the best lighting.

CLOCKWISE FROM TOP LEFT Leah, 2, and Greg Jones, only minutes away from the parking lot, at the shores of Bow Lake (Courtesy Stacey Jones); approaching the top of the steep section alongside the canyon – Bow Glacier Falls is in the distant centre; Bow Lake is one of the Rockies' prettiest lakes; the hike out can be incredibly scenic.

A busier Bow Lake, later in the day. The bridge at the left is a favourite place for photos and kids.

1. Hike past Num-Ti-Jah Lodge and find the signed Bow Glacier Falls trail at the west end of a parking area for guests of the lodge. Before doing that, though, you may wish to explore the worthwhile trail at the end of the parking lot on the left (south) side, which goes directly to the lakeshore for some outstanding views and scenery. You may have to return to the parking lot to then find the start of the main trail, past the lodge.

2. Once on the Bow Glacier Falls trail, hike for 3 km, around the lake, over two sets of gravel flats and up the right side of a deep canyon. This section is quite steep, and there are sections where a slip down the left side would be very bad. Hang onto the young ones.

3. After the canyon section, you soon reach a sign for the Alpine Club of Canada Bow Hut. Keep going straight, eventually arriving at the hanging valley where Bow Glacier Falls sits.

4. Descend into the valley and hike on rockier terrain to the base of the falls. There is much terrain to explore around the base of the falls if desired. Thankfully, most of the rock does not get slippery when wet, but extreme caution is still required if you choose to let the kids scramble up to higher terrain near the waterfall. Return the same way you came in.

41. PEYTO LAKE VIEWPOINTS

*A super easy and short interpretive walk
to a magnificent view of colourful Peyto Lake.*

LOCATION

Drive west on Highway 1, past Lake Louise, and take the Highway 93 turnoff (Exit 7) towards Jasper. Drive about 41 km and turn left into the Bow Summit parking lot.

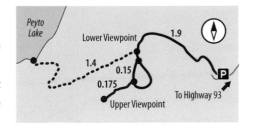

DISTANCE

1.9 km return

ELEVATION GAIN

50 m

DIFFICULTY

Easy, recommended for all; paved trail.

SEASON

Summer and early fall.

OF SPECIAL INTEREST FOR CHILDREN

Combine this trip with **42. Bow Summit Lookout Site** (next) for great views of both lakes. The lower viewpoint is usually very crowded; the upper viewpoint less so.

1. The paved trail starts at the north end of the parking lot and is easy to follow. Stop to read the interpretive information panels along the way. Follow the trail for about 500 m to the potentially very crowded lower viewing platform and a wonderful view of the turquoise waters of Peyto Lake.

CLOCKWISE FROM TOP What a view – and only ten minutes from the parking lot – some think the lake looks a ghost, some a dog – ask your kids what they think; a couple at the upper viewpoint checks out the view towards the magnificent Wapta Icefield; Gavin Emanuel, 3, takes in the view from the upper viewpoint (Courtesy Katy Emanuel).

2. Continue following the paved trail, soon reaching a three-way junction and an "Explore" sign. This is the beginning of the interpretive loop as well as the gateway to the Bow Summit hike. Take the right fork and hike about 150 m to the first interpretive panel. Look for an unsigned, unpaved trail branching off to the right. Follow this trail for about 175 m (at first ascending and then descending) to the rocky upper viewpoint. As well as enjoying another magnificent and slightly better view of Peyto Lake, you may even get to enjoy some solitude here!

3. Return to the paved trail and continue along the counter clockwise interpretive loop, eventually retuning to the "Explore" sign. Note that you will encounter signs for the Bow Summit Lookout trail and the trailhead along the loop. If you would like to extend your day, see **42. Bow Summit Lookout Site** (next trip). Otherwise, return to the parking lot the same way you came in or consider another trip extension that takes you closer to Peyto Lake (**Going Farther: Down to Peyto Lake** below).

Going Farther: Down to Peyto Lake

Be one of the few hearty souls to venture all the way down to the shores of the lake. Gaining all that elevation back is the crux of the trip!

DISTANCE
Add 2.8 km return

ELEVATION LOSS/GAIN
Add 260 m

DIFFICULTY
Strenuous, recommended for children aged 10 and older.

1. From the lower viewpoint, continue along the paved trail for a short distance, looking for the trail heading down on the right side.

Five hearty souls enjoy the lakeshore.

2. Follow this steep trail all the way down to the lake, first through forest and then down an avalanche slope.

3. Explore the shores of the lake as desired and then slowly grind your way back up to the viewpoint. Return the way you came in.

42. BOW SUMMIT LOOKOUT SITE

To complement the great view of Peyto Lake, continue up to this former lookout site for an equally enthralling view of Bow Lake.

LOCATION
Drive west on Highway 1, past Lake Louise, and take the Highway 93 turnoff (Exit 7) towards Jasper. Drive about 41 km and turn left into the Bow Summit parking lot.

To Highway 93

DISTANCE
7.4 km return

ELEVATION GAIN
245 m; high point: 2315 m

DIFFICULTY
Moderate, recommended for children aged six and older; good, gently graded trail throughout.

SEASON
Summer and early fall.

OF SPECIAL INTEREST FOR CHILDREN
Most people, families included, take on this hike in conjunction with Peyto Lake Viewpoints (trip **41**, previous). Note that the trail is Chariot / jogging-stroller friendly when dry.

1. Follow the instructions for **41. Peyto Lake Viewpoints**. You will find the trailhead to Bow Summit a short distance around the loop trail, a few hundred metres past the turnoff to the upper viewpoint, assuming you have hiked the loop in a counter clockwise direction

FROM TOP The view of Bow Lake and the surrounding mountains is the feature highlight of this trip; entering the superb environs around Bow Summit.

The scramblers' option to reach the rock face above.

2. From the trail sign, follow the wide trail for 2.9 km to a small, elevated, open area with an awesome view of Bow Lake. Return the way you came in or continue with an added scramble in step 3.

3. For the budding scrambler, follow the very steep scree trail from the open area up to the rock face above. The view is only slightly better, but undertake this scramble for the exercise and feeling of accomplishment for the kids. However, this section is only for kids who are comfortable on steep, loose scree.

FROM TOP **Bow Glacier Falls, page 144**, perfect lake reflections often occur early in the morning; **Bow Summit Lookout Site, page 151**, at elevations around 2300 m, snow often persists into July.

IMPORTANT CONTACTS

Kananaskis Country Trail Report » albertaparks.ca/parks/kananaskis/
kananaskis-country/advisories-public-safety/trail-reports
Tel: 403.678.3136

Barrier Lake Information Centre
Tel: 403.673.3985

Banff National Park Information Centre »
pc.gc.ca/eng/pn-np/ab/banff/visit
224 Banff Avenue, Banff Tel: 403.762.1550

Lake Louise Visitor Centre
Village of Lake Louise, next to Samson Mall
Tel: 403.522.3833 Trails office: 403.522.1264.

Emergency
Tel: 911

ACKNOWLEDGMENTS

*A huge thank you to Tanya Koob for photos,
invaluable information and inspiration. Thank you to
Gillean and Tony Daffern for paving the way for so many
of us in the Canadian Rockies. Also to Lynda Pianosi and
Brenda Kurtz Lenko for authoring their family hiking
guidebooks. And thank you to the following individuals
for their photo contributions: Par Boora, Sonny Bou,
Dan Carreiro, Matthew Clay, Karen Christison, Vern Dewit,
Amelie Doucet, John Doucet, Katy Emanuel, Alyssa Erickson,
Brianne Hobbs, Matthew Hobbs, Ian Hunt, Kathy Hunt,
Greg Jones, Stacey Jones, Mark Koob, Zeljko Kozomara,
Nicole Lisafeld, Scott McLean, Mark Nugara, Artur Opalinski,
Brigid Meegan Scott, Bob Spirko, Marko Stavric,
Shannon Young and Amy Wong.*